D0188434

The Proverbs 31 Lady

A N D

Other Impossible Dreams

MARSHA DRAKE

BETHANY HOUSE PUBLISHERS
MINNEAPOLIS, MINNESOTA 55438
A Division of Bethany Fellowship, Inc.

Scripture quotations marked NASB are from the New American Standard Bible, © The Lockman Foundation 1960, 1962, 1963, 1968, 1971, 1972, 1973, 1975, 1977. Used by permission.

Verses marked AMP are taken from The Amplified Bible, Old Testament, copyright © 1962, 1964 by Zondervan Publishing House. Used by permission.

Verses marked TLB are taken from *The Living Bible*, copyright 1971 by Tyndale House Publishers, Wheaton, IL. Used by permission.

Scripture quotations marked AMP are from the Amplified New Testament, © The Lockman Foundation 1954, 1958. Used by permission.

Verses marked KJV are from the King James Version of the Bible.

Copyright © 1984
Marsha Drake
All Rights Reserved

Published by Bethany House Publishers
A Division of Bethany Fellowship, Inc.
6820 Auto Club Road, Minneapolis, Minnesota 55438

Printed in the United States of America

Library of Congress Cataloging in Publication Data

Drake, Marsha.
    The Proverbs 31 Lady and other impossible dreams.

    1. Women—Conduct of life. 2. Bible. O.T. Proverbs XXXI, 10–31—Meditations. 3. Drake, Marsha. I. Title. II. Title: Proverbs thirty-one Lady and other impossible dreams.
BJ1610.D7   1984   248.8′43   84–6453
ISBN 0–87123–595–1

5.95

The Proverbs 31 Lady

AND

Other Impossible Dreams

Dedicated to:

Bill
Matt
Mike

Foreword

Imagination is probably the most neglected quality of each person's life. The reason is that most of us refuse to be ourselves. We want to be somebody else—to imitate the colorful achievers we hear on cassettes and read about in books rather than the unique person which God created.

This is the story of a captive housewife haunted by the original liberated woman, that visionary wife, entrepreneur, and actualizer of Proverbs 31. It is an odyssey of guilt and contrived glory in a vain effort to imitate Her, to soar like Her, and to be as efficient, as worthy, as girded with strength and as wise.

As this one frail modern woman seeks to brighten the corner of her world in the shadow of a mighty outcropping of rock called "The Chief," she makes an exciting discovery. The more she tries, and fails, to be like Her the more she becomes Her through the power of the Lord Jesus Christ.

Unaware of the changes within herself, she is only aware of the changes in other people—especially her family. And in the end it is her husband, the one she thinks she has failed the most, who reveals the truth to her:

There are many fine women in the world
but you are the best of them all.

This story is feminine mystique as God ordained it, the liberated woman explained from the biblical perspective, the search for self-esteem outlined for the humblest reader. One will find in this book the meaning of existence with eternity in view and help for real and imagined hurts.

Norman B. Rohrer

Preface

Proverbs 31 has been both a marvelous model for the Christian wife and the cause of more guilt for her than anything else. When those verses become the pattern for a do-it-yourself project, frustration, guilt, and disillusionment can only result. When seen as what the power of the Holy Spirit can accomplish, those same verses are winsome and hope-filled.

Marsha Drake has caught the difference between the two ways of reading Proverbs 31 with a delightful touch of humor and that kind of insight that says, "This comes from personal experience." Many aspiring Christian housewives will see themselves in Marsha's words. Moreover, Christian husbands will be a bit more understanding and cooperative with the Holy Spirit's workings as they follow this Christian woman's adventure of faith.

Of particular delight is our personal remembrance of the author when we first knew her as a high school girl and daughter of a faithful and loving pastor. Reading between the lines, it would appear that God has indeed done that miracle of making a fine woman into that even-finer Proverbs 31 woman-in-Christ. Knowing Marsha, we suspect that *The Proverbs 31 Lady and Other Impossible Dreams* is autobiographical as well as being brilliantly written.

We salute you, Marsha.

Ralph Osborne
On behalf of both
Lloyd Ogilvie and myself

Table of Contents

SPRING

1 / *Awakening*

I was lying in bed reading my Bible and eating a large bowl of buttery popcorn, trying not to get grease stains on the pages, when I found the description of a woman of all women. My husband's snores and relaxed face assured me that I wasn't bothering him with the light, so I read on.

She was unbelievable. I couldn't believe my eyes, but there it was, beginning at verse ten—the Proverbs 31 Lady. . . .

"Could anyone really live like that?" I wondered out loud. I laid the Bible on the nightstand, snuggled into my pillow, and fell asleep. And I dreamed that I was She. I was beautiful, I was celestial, I was . . .

"Hey, Mom, did you get the new toothpaste yet?" The voice was close—too close. I could feel warm air on my face.

Bolting upright in bed, I yelled, "Asleep! What am I doing asleep? Where is your father?"

I beheld the face of our youngest son, George, blue eyes shining with expectation, braces exposed, hair going twenty different directions. "He said he'd just have some toast and coffee. He said not to wake you. He said—"

"You mean he's already gone to work?" I narrowed my gaze, incredulous at my son's lack of sensitivity to my low self-esteem—not up at the crack of dawn, not ready to greet the day and fill my husband with warm food before he left for work.

Being up was the bare minimum of responsibility in my book.

Nervously twiddling his toothbrush, my baby, my own, stuck out his chin. "He said to be nice to you this morning, and that's what I'm gonna do."

I tried not to snap. I took a deep breath and calmed myself. "What did you mean—new toothpaste?" I inquired, trying to smile good-naturedly.

Patiently, as though explaining it to his pet frog, he crossed his arms and leaned on one leg. I was amazed he didn't topple over. "I told you yesterday, this stuff we've got rusts my braces." He chomped his teeth a few times for emphasis.

I groaned and heaved back the comforter. "It won't rust your braces; but, if I'm lucky, it might give you lockjaw."

He hung his head and stared at the floor. He started to turn away.

"No, come back," I said quickly. "I didn't mean it. I wouldn't want anything to happen to you. It's just that I was dreaming . . . But I'm awake now. Okay?" My eyes pleaded for his understanding. I hated myself for hurting my small boy who was just trying to be cooperative about his braces.

He looked up and gave me an affectionate grin. "Hey, Mom? My teacher says the flouride in this toothpaste will kill me. Will I get sick if I use this stuff?" He looked down at the crumpled tube in his hand, blue goo covering his right thumb.

I swung my legs over the side of the bed and groped for my slippers with my toes. My dream would have to wait.

I padded out to the kitchen to put the kettle on for coffee.

"Mom?" he said as he danced around, "I feel daring this morning. I'm going to take a chance and use it. What do you think?" His face was smeared with blue from ear to ear and foam ran down his chin.

"Do that," I replied, heading back toward my room to get dressed. "But hurry up, or you'll be late for school."

I closed the door to my room. Taking my time getting my clothes on and brushing my hair, I groped through my memory banks, trying to recall the fantasy my son's voice had shattered. Disquiet settled upon me. What if I couldn't remember it?

Blank. My mind was blank. *Maybe if I lie down again*, I thought hopefully, getting back into bed fully dressed. *Sometimes that works.* I stared at the ceiling, feeling ridiculous.

I sat up in desperation and glanced over at the clock on my night table. An empty popcorn bowl stared back at me. "You're probably the culprit!" I said with a sneer to the silent vessel.

I quickly began to make the bed. Deciding against it due to lack of time, I threw back the covers and fluffed the pillows. Horrible guilt twisted me as I saw the imprint of a head still on my husband's pillow. *How could I have done it again? A godly wife should at least be up in the morning,* I accused.

Sadly I picked up my popcorn bowl, the salt shaker, a half-empty juice glass and opened the door.

Realizing that I'd been outdone by Her was painful. Just at that moment I remembered my discovery of Her last night and my dream about being the Proverbs 31 Lady. But of course it had been only the popcorn before bed—my morning had just proved I could *never* measure up. I trudged toward the kitchen picking up scraps of paper and bits of dog fur and lint off the carpet along the way. I heard an ominous crunch under my foot and looked down to see a partially chewed dog biscuit which I'd just ground into the rug. "Can't anybody in the house except me ever pick up anything?" I griped to everyone, but nobody was listening. Specimen, John Jr.'s dog, a huge, black part-Labrador part-elephant, was safely outside, out of the reach of my wrath.

"What's for breakfast?" Grinning broadly, the toothbrusher arrived in the kitchen. Turning his metallic smile on me, he pushed past en route to the refrigerator. "Gotta get a carrot for my guinea pig. Ben likes lots of carrots!" he explained.

"And you get to eat Pow-Wow," I replied. I struggled up the kitchen stool to reach for the new hot cereal loaded with vitamins, minerals, and probably a bit of sawdust.

"Pow-Wow? Yuk! I hate it!!" His mouth curled around his dental work.

"How do you know? You've never tasted it," announced John Jr., my oldest, his blue eyes glazed at the sight of food.

I leaped off the stool, landing heavily, and deposited the Pow-Wow box on the stove.

"Kettle is boiling dry," stated fifteen-year-old John Jr. As he reached over to flip off the burner, he knocked the cereal box over.

"Oh, no," I moaned, trying to stay calm.

"Mom?" My middle son, Joe, hurled his voice from the center of the living room rug. "What's for breakfast?"

Forcing my mind to "condition blue," I replied unperturbed, "Aren't you dressed yet?"

"No, I'm not dressed yet," he shot back. "It's these stupid socks! Where did you get such dumb socks?" His accusing voice raised my blood pressure thirty points.

"Mom, there's cereal on the stove," John Jr. reminded me.

"I know," I answered through clenched teeth. "I'll get it later."

"I think I should clean it up now. It looks like sawdust, and sawdust catches fire very quickly." His tone was authoritative. "Should I get the vacuum?"

"You should go to your room," I snapped, slamming the kitchen counter with my hand to punctuate my remark.

Unprepared for my blast, he shrugged. "Well, I was just trying to help, like Dad said," and he marched righteously out of the kitchen.

"Was *everybody* up before I was this morning?" I muttered under my breath. I rolled my eyes heavenward and thought, *At any moment, I am going to scream, and then they are going to come and get me . . .*

"Mom?"

"Yeeeaaaaaaah!" I shrieked.

Instantly the room cleared. The whole main floor of the house was suddenly empty.

When I had cooled down somewhat, I invited them all to come and eat their breakfast, whereupon I explained that I'd been a little out of sorts and asked them to forgive my short temper.

They wouldn't eat their Pow-Wow.

"Look, kids," I reasoned. "This stuff is *good* for you."

They replied by crunching toast and gulping orange juice and milk. Like a trained army, they, in unison, ignored their Pow-Wow.

"All right, you guys," I cajoled, "you may have a little more sugar."

They eagerly covered their three bowls of lukewarm cereal with a layer of granulated white. And ate the top layer.

"May we go now, Mom?" They asked hopefully almost in one voice.

"No. You may not go," I snapped. "And I may never let you out of this house again! You will eat your cereal right now, or you will sit there until it rots, and then you will still have to eat it!" Having made my pronouncement, I began to clear the table of everything except the three bowls of cold, solidified, weeping cereal.

They ate it.

She wouldn't have threatened them, my mind accused. "When She speaks, Her words are wise, and kindness is the rule for everything She says."[1]

It was time for school and the boys quietly got their coats. I had the feeling they expected me to burn them at the stake if they angered me again.

"Look, kids," I said apologetically as I put on my plaid jacket, "I'm really not all bad. It's just that I had a strange dream, and I can't seem to get a handle on it."

"I know how it is," responded my forgiving youngest. "Maybe it'll come back to you after we're gone."

"Right," I answered, while my thoughts whispered, *It's already back . . .*

"Or . . . I know!" His eyes sparkled with excitement. "Just ask Daddy! He'll know what to do." His expression was angelic.

The other two boys nodded their forgiveness and approval, and I resolved to get to the bottom of my strange dream that very morning. *Why lose my grip because of a silly illusion?* I asked myself. One thing I was certain of, however: I wasn't going to tell my husband John—not yet—and for a lot of reasons that nobody, least of all me, understood.

We piled into the car and began our daily drive to school.

When I rolled down my car window, I knew my sinuses would be killing me later; the morning air was fragranced by spring pollens. Driving down the street with the boys still combing their hair and complaining about broken shoelaces, I noticed the early morning mists rolling off various-colored rooftops. Sunshine peeked above the mountains which ringed our small town. The sight was gentle to my mind.

I dropped each boy at his respective spot in front of two schools and savored a moment of peace before I turned the car around for home. I felt as though I were in a capsule floating in outer space—until a horn honked and a school bus nearly side-swiped me. "Those dreadful school buses—road hogs," I mut-tered angrily under my breath. "Oughta be driving tanks."

Hitting the accelerator hard, my car bolted out of the way and sped down the street toward home. Careening into the driveway, I almost ran over the little white picket fence that always fell sideways into the drive. Hauling myself out of the car, I trudged over, restored it to its original position—crooked—and watched it fall slowly sideways. "Hope. That's what I need to make it in this world." I was addressing a dying asparagus plant.

Suddenly an idea struck me. The cloud of gloom which had hung over my head since waking lifted a little as I thought of it. *I'll stare at the Chief for a bit—for inspiration.*

Quickly I walked to the center of my backyard, looked up at my favorite mountain, and said, "Hi, Chief." It was a moment of singular tranquillity amid a sea of chaos.

My eyes feasted upon the sight of the Stawamus Chief Moun-tain. It stood (actually it lay down on its back so that the chief looked at the heavens) majestically in all its grandeur, forming the profile of a sleeping Indian chief etched against the cloudless sky. Just knowing I was confronted by the second largest rock in the world gave me goose bumps of awe. I felt an emotion stir deep within me. Could it be hope?

I was the only one in town who liked the Chief. Everybody else crabbed, growled, and complained because it cast its shadow—in the early morning (spring), the late morning (fall), and the rest of the day (winter)—over the entire town. Not only did it put the residents in the "twilight zone," it stopped all the clouds before they headed west—thereby causing tons of rain to fall annually. The fog in the spring, and the fog during the other three seasons of the year, should have given the colossus an ethereal effect, but it didn't. My neighbors hated living in opaque soup. Therefore, they hated my favorite mountain.

It was the civic depression caused by the Chief that caused me to look for a way to brighten up my corner of the world while living in perpetual twilight. Observing my neighbors fall into the I-hate-the-Chief (therefore, I-hate-the-world) trap, I decided that I would find a message of hope for the world. Realizing that I was only one small woman, I decided to find a message of hope for women only.

And that is how I came across Proverbs 31, and HER.

My husband John, bless his dear heart, had been puzzled by my strange behavior since my discovery, and that just made it worse. My personality, like a yo-yo, was up one day and down the next. I wished with all my heart that I had never come across Her, but that only increased my self-reproach. *She* was in the Bible; therefore, She had to be important.

Standing in the center of my backyard, my face toward the Chief, I stretched a finger toward his nose, which faced skyward. "You know an awful lot, don't you? You've been lying there so long and you've watched so many people." Wholly engrossed in the mood of the moment, I closed my eyes tightly and continued my soliloquy with the Chief.

"What are you doing?" The voice of my neighbor, Elvira Shanks, pierced my reverie.

Embarrassed, I turned slowly toward her while madly collecting my thoughts. "I'm praying for rain," I replied calmly, "I think."

"Why on earth would you want more rain, Martha? Don't we get more than our share already?" She kicked the ground with her foot and dislodged a piece of sod.

"That's negative thinking," I responded smoothly.

"That's the only thinking possible if you live next to that thing you were just talking to," she shot back, gesturing toward the Chief. So she hadn't bought the praying story.

"Any particular reason you wanted to see me?" I asked, to change the subject.

"Just wondered if you wanted some strawberry runners for

your garden," she answered matter-of-factly.

"Thanks for asking, but not today," I replied.

She left soon, and I stood alone again. I felt so foolish, discouraged, and hopeless. Looking back up at the Chief, I said softly, "How much do you think she heard? After this I'll talk to you from my living room window."

Clouds hovered over the mountains. They matched the gloom that now hit me full force as I pondered the reality of my existence. I was, after all, only an ordinary woman with a neighbor who thought I was crazy, a totally unreachable dream, a bewildered husband, a sink full of dirty dishes, and three ordinary kids trying to grow up in a troubled world. *Me? Be like HER? Who am I kidding?* The air felt cold, and the earth seemed unfriendly. A shiver crept across my shoulders.

Thinking again of my neighbor, Elvira, I tried kicking the ground with my toe and felt a searing pain shoot up my leg. "Humph," I complained. "I can't even kick the ground without—

"But wait! Neither can she!" I looked triumphantly up at my beloved mountain. "Nobody can kick at life without getting hurt. I'm not going to quit before I even begin, Chief."

Standing on one foot in the middle of my backyard, I glanced high above the Chief and caught the first glimmer of sunshine just as it broke through the clouds, sending streams of light that touched my favorite monolith's nose. Inspiration flooded my soul; and as I limped toward the house, Elvira could have heard me saying, "I won't give up. Not yet. Tomorrow I'll be up *before dawn*, just like Her!"

2 / Nightmare

Everything was quiet under my comforter—too quiet for a weekday morning. Why wasn't I hearing the stereo, the kids, or the dog? Why wasn't I hearing any snoring?

Ahhhhh, no! my mind screamed at me. *Morning! I've missed the dawn! I've missed everything.* When my muddy brain could muster some nerve impulses to my arm, I felt for my husband's side of the bed. My heart sank. *Cold. Stone cold.* Still groggy, I listened for sounds in the house. *Nothing.*

"Kids! Kids! Get up! Everybody up!" I shouted. "You're airing your beds today—don't bother to make them. And hurry, you've got five minutes . . . "

The smell of food wafted down the hall.

"Breakfast's cooking, Mom," yelled the oldest. "Don't worry. Dad told us yesterday we're big enough to take care of ourselves until you're feeling better."

My unkind response about how I was "feeling" was smothered when the smoke detector let out an ear-piercing blast.

"Fire!" I screamed. "Fire! Quick! Head for the door!" Running full tilt toward the kitchen, I ran smack into Joe, who was running for the front door.

"Owwwww!" we yelled in unison.

"It's all right now," announced my oldest, junior John, wiping his hands with my best dish towel. "I poured baking soda on the flames."

23

"Oh," I replied weakly, leaning against the wall. "What time is it?"

"It's okay," added my youngest coming down the hall carrying his toothbrush dripping with blue foam. "We've still got ten minutes until the first bell rings." He walked calmly toward the bathroom.

"Ten minutes!" I screeched. "I'm standing here in my bathrobe, and you tell me it's okay because we've still got ten minutes?"

"And, by the way," continued young George unperturbed, "didya get the new toothpaste yet?" I wondered how he could possibly be so dense. He had less than five minutes to eat, get washed and dressed, and be out the door with his shoes on. I made a mental note: *Teach youngest son to observe the passage of time.*

"Forget your teeth," I retorted, following him.

"How can I? Daddy said—" He was interrupted in mid-sentence as I whirled into the bathroom to weigh myself. No matter what happened, I weighed in. He looked confused and crestfallen as he carefully placed his toothbrush in the holder and put away the toothpaste. I noted that too: *Explain to George that life is not always fair, and try to decipher my horrible conduct to John, my poor husband.*

"How could I have gained five pounds overnight?" I queried the scale. In a daze I fled to the kitchen to try to throw something together for breakfast. Whatever had been cooking on the stove was unsalvageable. Trying to ignore the baking soda mess, I checked the clock on the kitchen wall. Too late for any more cooking.

"Hurry, everybody. How'd you like to try that new ice cream we made last night?" Hating myself, I madly scooped large helpings of chocolate-cherry-almond ice cream into their cereal bowls.

"This is great, Mom," they enthused as they wolfed it down. I decided not to look. Remembering that I wasn't dressed, I dashed to the bedroom and frantically threw on some clothes. Figuring that shoes would take too long, I convinced myself that moccasin slippers would be good enough. I pushed down any guilty thoughts about what kind of mother does this sort of thing and sprinted for my sunglasses, purse, and car keys.

The ice cream euphoria had not lasted; all the boys were out of sorts as they piled into the car. I heard the irritation in Joe's voice; "Get your finger out of my eye!" But I was proud when George answered, "I'm sorry."

"Must be doing something right," I muttered as I backed out of the driveway.

I turned around in my seat and smiled at them all. "Good morning, guys. How did you sleep?"

"What happened?" They said it almost in unison.

"The stereo didn't work," I explained. "Isn't it a lovely morning? Smell that air!"

"Why didn't the stereo work?" asked George.

"Maybe the timer didn't come on," I answered, half-hearing him.

"But why didn't Daddy get us up like he did yesterday morning?" He was insistent.

"You ask too many questions," I replied smoothly.

I knew why Daddy didn't get them up. I'd promised him that I'd be up for sure this morning. As the newly elected mayor of our town, he had to attend an early morning meeting before he began his teaching day at the high school. I didn't bother to ask myself why I hadn't gotten up. I was too miserable.

Blue-eyes-with-braces-George gave up trying to get a straight answer out of me and settled down for the ride.

The pure blue sky sparkled against the mountaintops, and my emotions lifted as I drove silently along. It was a nice morning for a drive—sunshine, clean air (the pulpmill was on a shutdown), and no traffic. I dropped the two youngest boys off at the corner near the elementary school and proceeded toward the high school.

"Look!" I said to my oldest. "Do you see that small boy lying beside the road?"

I noticed two older boys standing near the fallen child.

"Uh, oh," I continued, "those two bullies are holding wooden swords. I wonder if the little one is hurt. What do you think?"

I slowed down to ten miles per hour.

"I've got to get to school, Mom." I was startled by the tone of his voice and incensed by his impassive face.

"What did you say?" My query was icy.

"I said I've got to get to school." My fifteen-year-old son's eyes shot a challenging look.

I glared at him, then I pushed down the accelerator hard. The car leaped forward.

"And what about being a good Samaritan?" I yelled! He shrank back into his seat. I told him at the top of my lungs that I was a Christian, and that it was my job to see that I was a good helper, and last week a neighbor boy had nearly lost his eye from a sharp stick wound. I concluded with something like, "If we can't help others in their time of need, what is the point of living?"

"I'm sorry," he said simply. "You'd better slow down, Mom."

"I'm sorry, too," I responded, deflated, as I braked for a stop sign.

"I wonder what did happen to the stereo," he murmured.

He looked very grown up, and his blue eyes glowed with maturity. I could almost see his father a young man again, and a wave of warmth flowed over me. I had a wonderful family. I resolved to treat them all better for the rest of my life. . . .

I dropped off John Jr. and turned the car around toward home.

Driving past the spot where the boys had been, I slowed for a look but they were gone. Either somebody else had helped the injured boy, or he hadn't been hurt.

They might have just been playing, I rationalized.

When I arrived back at the house, I skipped saying "Hi" to the Chief. My morning's performance made me too miserable.

As I cleaned up the mess from the ice cream breakfast and the charred stove burner, my churning thoughts tormented me. *How could it have happened? How could I have actually yelled, and raced down the street like a maniac?* Instead of my being up before dawn, everyone nearly missed school, my poor mate went to work without even a good-bye kiss (never mind a decent breakfast), and I was behaving like a nagging shrew.

SHE would be up before dawn. The thought bounced around inside my brain. Feeling discouraged, I considered the situation.

"First I am going to tell John exactly what is bothering me," I promised myself. "And then I'll fix things so that we can have some time alone together. But for now, I'm going to find something constructive to do. I need to keep myself busy so that I can stop worrying about this." I thought for a moment.

Suddenly I knew what I needed. "The garden!" I said it aloud, shocking myself with the volume.

Quickly I finished wiping the kitchen counter, did a once-over around the rest of the house, and hurried outside.

I stared dismally at the weed patch. "Well, no time like the present," I said bravely. I fell to my knees and began to pull weeds. After a while I discovered that some of the roots were too strong to pull. I scurried to get the garden shovel and began to dig.

"Oh, so you're getting ready to plant, are you?" I welcomed Elvira's voice—my green-thumbed neighbor.

"Good. You're here. I was thinking I'd get some strawberry plants in; that is, if you have time to bring them back and help me." The fresh air and sunshine washed away my crankiness.

"Sure." She looked around the weed patch (now showing some usable soil) with a practiced eye. "Be right back."

As I watched her stroll toward her greenhouse, my dream lady flashed before my eyes.

" . . . with her own hands she plants a vineyard. . . . She is energetic, a hard worker. . . . She works far into the night!"[2]

I dug with new vigor and determination.

The rest of the morning was uneventful. I planted nine strawberry plants. The going was rough; the ground was hard and full of rocks. Elvira had to go downtown right in the middle of planting, but she gave me good directions before she left.

I managed to position the remaining strawberry runners with their roots under the soil, and their center crowns toward the sky. Then I gave them a drink.

A sense of well-being swept over me as I surveyed my accomplishments. The only cloud on my horizon, which I felt I handled quite well, was that I would have to wait at least a year before I saw any berries.

Back in the house, I poured myself a cup of coffee and took an inventory of the day.

"*She* gets up before dawn." I didn't make it. "*She* prepares breakfast." Ice cream!

The telephone rang.

"Hello?" I queried.

"Hi, honey," came the reply. The deep voice of my husband sounded soothing as he asked hopefully, "Did you manage all right this morning?"

"No, and I'd like to talk to you about that later."

"Okay." He sounded relieved. "Glad you're all right. I'll be a little late tonight, so don't worry."

As we said our good-byes, I felt warmed by his care and concern. My hopes began to soar. *Maybe I'm stewing around about nothing,* I thought.

I went back to my list with enthusiasm. "*She* plans the day's work." The day was nearly over (zero for that one). Tension lines crept along my eyebrows, and I smoothed them with my index fingers. "*She* inspects a field." Sort of. "*She* plants a vineyard." Yes—strawberries. "*She* is a hard worker." That one required some thought.

If I used the scientific definition of "work," that would mean something had to be *moved*. One could push and pull a rock, I'd learned while in school (and I did move rocks out of the garden); but, if that rock didn't move, however (according to somebody's law), then no "work" was accomplished. I decided that since I did heft some stones that morning, I deserved one hundred percent for being a hard worker. *Hurray!* I thought, rubbing my nose with my wrist.

But how can I haul boulders, stay up late working far into the night, and still get up in the morning? I puzzled.

You can't! My brain exclaimed.

Obviously I faced an impossible dilemma. How did She do it? I allowed myself to grit my teeth one more time as I recalled my recurring dream and today's nightmare.

"Onward!" I admonished myself. "Such comparison thinking will get you nowhere except down."

I heard pounding at the back door and shouts of, "Mom! We're home!" Lunchtime. I bolted for the kitchen.

Lunch over, I felt calm. And then it happened. A dream attack. Shivering slightly, I pulled my Bible out of the drawer of my night table and compulsively opened it to Proverbs 31. I needed inspiration. Quickly I scanned the verses, trying to find something that I could do to be like Her. "She sews . . ."

There it was! Maybe getting up before dawn should be replaced by something more lofty—something creative! I couldn't wait to get started. I would begin to *sew*!

3 / Sewing

"She lays her hands to the spindle, and her hands hold the distaff."[3]

My eyes opened wide. The word "distaff" literally leaped off the page at me.

Visions of *me* creating elegant designs paraded before my imagination. I could see myself greeting my husband at the door, clothed in a flowing gown of alabaster white, accented by gold trim and purple braid. Pearls adorned my neck. It was perfect!

Like a lightning bolt, a rude thought exploded my reverie— *What is a distaff?*

Blowing some dust off my dog-eared dictionary, I opened it and flipped the pages until I came to "distaff." "Humm," I said, reading with interest, "it's the staff for holding the flax, tow, or wool in spinning. But what's a tow?" I kept reading.

"Woman's work . . . "

I slammed the book shut! Why, why, why did it have to be *woman's work*? Why couldn't I be a carpenter like my aptitude test in high school had shown? Why did I want to be like Her?

Once I had calmed myself, I remembered that if She could sew, I could sew. It didn't exactly make me feel better, but it did get me back on the track. I wasn't there for long, though. I didn't know *how* to sew! Not knowing how to begin, doing what I didn't know how to do, sent me straight to the living room window to stare at the Chief for some inspiration.

No sooner had I placed my vision upon the Chief than another thought blasted my brain. *SHE doesn't stare; SHE sews!*

"Right!" I said aloud. Refusing to escape by daydreaming instead of working, I pulled myself away from the window, reached for my purse and car keys, and marched straight to the car. *I know I need material*, I thought, backing out of the driveway. *That much I do know . . .*

"There's nothing to it. You'll do fine." The fabric-shop owner's assurance did not match the concern in her eyes.

After three hours in her store, Viv might have had reason to be troubled by my potential. Instead she queried politely, "Have you ever done any sewing?"

"I made a pair of pajamas once, and some curtains for the bathroom. Guess that won't help much though, will it?"

"That will help, I'm sure." Patiently she toured me around the store. Her nimble fingers plucked out a bolt of white from among the rest.

"I *love* white!" I exclaimed recalling my earlier vision.

"It's quite nice," she replied, ignoring me. "It's a blend of polyester and cotton. Very practical for everyday wear. No ironing at all."

"I could make a dress out of this, I bet," I responded with enthusiasm.

"Let's make a blouse first, shall we?" Her smile seemed a bit forced.

"Oh, certainly," I agreed. I noticed a diamond pattern running through the material. She was right. It wouldn't make a good dress.

She helped me choose a pattern for a blouse. She said it would be easy, and I believed her.

By the time I bought thread, buttons, and a small "How to Sew" pamphlet, I wanted to quit. But I went ahead anyway, encouraging myself all the way until the thought hit that She could probably make a blouse before breakfast.

Hurrying home, I again ignored the Chief. I was going to do this little project all by myself.

Laying out the slippery white cloth onto my slick kitchen table presented the first challenge. The material just wouldn't stay put. Everytime I got set to cut, the scissors slipped, or the pattern moved. Scared of ruining the material, I called Viv.

"Viv?" I caught her just before her lunch break. "Viv, I can't cut this material. Either it slips or the pattern slides. I just thought maybe I should call you and let you know so that you don't sell the rest of the fabric on that bolt—"

"What kind of shears are you using?" Her tone seemed curt.

"Just scissors," I shot back. "I've had them for years. What's wrong with that? It's the material that's moving, not the scissors."

I heard a hurt silence. "Whatever you wish."

"No! Wait, Viv. Maybe I need new scissors. Do you think I need new scissors?"

"I wouldn't want you to think I'm forcing you to buy new shears, dear."

"Wait for lunch, please." My tone pleaded for mercy. I couldn't lose my only ally. "I'm on my way."

"Very well," she responded. I could tell it was all right, though, when she chuckled a little, "Hurry on down. My yogurt is melting."

I loathed myself all the way to town. How did I get into these things? But I was trying to become virtuous, not argumentative. I decided to apologize.

Breezing my way into the store, I announced, "Viv, thank you. I'm really sorry. Where are the scissors?"

An hour later I arrived home with a pair of sewing shears and a disgruntled spirit for losing most of the morning. "Oh, well," I reasoned to myself, "I should learn to be more friendly anyway."

Once back at the kitchen table, I watched in fascination as the dressmaking shears bit the material and sliced through it like butter. Viv was right. New scissors helped. Tiny beads of perspiration formed along my hairline as I completed the task.

Piling the freshly cut fabric onto the sewing machine, I sighed from the exhaustive effort. My back ached from the strain of holding a half-bent position for nearly two hours.

The telephone rang. "Aren't you coming to pick me up?" My oldest son sounded impatient.

"For what?" I responded placidly.

"Mom, are you okay? I mean, I only left a few hours ago for school." There was that tone again.

"Oh, no. School? Sorry." I left the telephone dangling from its cord and raced for the door.

"How do I get myself into these things?" I asked myself as I drove at breakneck speed toward the high school.

You asked that earlier, my mind replied.

I pulled up in front of the now-deserted building. There he stood. The only one in all the world still at school. Shame reddened my ears.

"Whatcha been doin', Mom?" John Jr. eyed me curiously.

"Sewing. I'm making a blouse. Sorry I'm late."

"I didn't know you could sew," he replied admiringly. Johnny threw his books in the backseat. "What's for supper?"

"Supper? Would you believe I forgot supper?" I tried to joke.

"I'd believe it," he agreed, laughing good-naturedly.

"Don't get smart," I snapped.

Utterly perplexed by my unhinged behavior, he stayed quiet the rest of the way home.

Since I had neglected to prepare supper, the boys and I ate hamburgers at a small Chinese restaurant just outside of town. Fortunately, hubby had a dinner meeting. Guilt over my day's performance nagged at me, my spirit was sore and my finger blistered.

"Where'd ya get the blister, Mom?" the voice of George inquired.

"She's not feeling well," replied John Jr.

"Nobody tells me anything," complained Joe.

This is not going according to plan, I thought.

By the time John appeared home, weary and looking for companionship, I was already sound asleep. And I was still in my dreams when he and the boys prepared their own breakfast and departed. Disappointment dragged me to the point of despair when I said good morning to an empty house. I felt certain they were trying to avoid me.

I realized fatigue had finished me. While washing the breakfast dishes, I discovered the smudge marks on the refrigerator door. I was elbow-deep in Scrub and Scour when the telephone rang.

"Hello?" I said suspiciously.

"This is the school calling. I wonder if you would meet your son at the medical clinic. He's going to be getting a couple of stitches." The monotone voice cared nothing for my emotions.

The worst part of the whole ordeal was that the school sent me to one clinic, and my son George to another! Three phone calls and one hour later, I found him bravely lying on a white cot talking about soccer to a stranger in white. It was not our usual clinic.

After seven stitches, one smudge-free refrigerator door, and thirty-five thousand frazzled nerves, I had assembled the blouse. It was 2:00 a.m.

It wasn't until the next morning that I discovered the collar was in backwards.

"Viv?" I called as I hurried into the store. The frantic tone in my voice grabbed her attention instantly. "I've put the collar in backwards!" I held it out to her.

"There, there, dear. Calm yourself. I'm certain it can be fixed." She appeared very concerned about me as she took the blouse out of my shaking hands and began clipping stitches.

The sound of the clipping finished me. I could again see my youngest covered in blood, his hand all red where he had tried to hold his eyebrow together. My muscles seemed to dissolve.

"Are you all right? Maybe you should just sit down while I do this." Viv's voice had a soothing effect on me. I sat in a daze and watched as she re-did the collar and pinned it in properly.

"You see," she instructed as she snipped, "most storemade garments aren't perfect either. I'm certain you've never checked the collar points to see if they match, have you?"

"Oh, no," I responded softly, "I never have."

"Well, then," she firmly packaged the blouse in brown paper, "do you suppose anyone will check the points on your blouse?"

"Oh, no," I replied dutifully.

The collar sewed in and looking rather similar to other collars I had seen, I tackled the sleeves. How on earth could one be expected to fit all that material into one small opening? The pattern instructions said *"ease* the material . . . " Somehow that word didn't seem to fit with all the grief I was having. Finally, lots of ripping and two not-quite-smooth sleeves later, I remembered someone telling me that the finishing touches take almost as long as the basic sewing.

I was unable to face it. "Who needs it?" I asked myself seriously. "Anyway," I reasoned, "taking a break will let my creativity incubate a little."

A month later I noticed a lot of dust collecting on the sewing machine. Afraid of clogging up the gears with dirt, I cleaned the machine thoroughly and doused it with a generous coat of oil. Cheerfully surveying the shining piece of machinery, I decided to finish the blouse. When I floored the accelerator to finish the hem in a hurry, a black polka-dot effect graced the edge of the white material and continued up the wall.

Frankly, I was sick of sewing.

"Honey," it was the voice of my husband, "I want you to know that I like the candlelight dinners we're having. Any special reason?" John looked extra handsome as he spoke.

How could I tell him I couldn't face the oil spots on the wall or on my soul? "Thank you, dear," I replied meekly.

The next day I put the blouse away unfinished in the bottom of the linen closet. Case closed—almost.

"Hey, Mom? When are you gonna wear your new blouse?" Joe's question at the dinner table grated on my already frazzled nervous system. I fled to the kitchen. As I left, I heard—"Not now, Joe" and "Why not?" and silence. I could imagine the stern look John had delivered to our middle son.

The next morning I couldn't resist looking up the word "distaff" again. The house quiet, the blouse buried, my curiosity got the better of me. "What does *that* mean—'a staff for holding the flax which is the woman's work or authority'?" Staring at the page in the old dictionary, I wondered how a woman derived any *authority* from winding wool. "I'm sick of 'distaff' too," I said to myself.

Straightening my shoulders, I walked to the picture window to gaze upon the Chief. "You see," I told him in growing excitement, "I now realize the error of my ways. I've been trying to be like Her from the blouse-side-in instead of the inside-out. Simple! I must find another way—"

Suddenly I knew! I almost skipped my way to the vacuum cleaner. Possibly the most important discovery of my entire existence had stormed its way into my skull. *I need to get spiritual*, I reasoned.

And how would I go about getting holy like Her? The answer, so simple, yet so satisfying, came out of my mouth in sugar sweet tones, "I'm going to attend a *Bible* study."

The blouse was out of my way and out of my thoughts. I knew spirituality would be a snap!

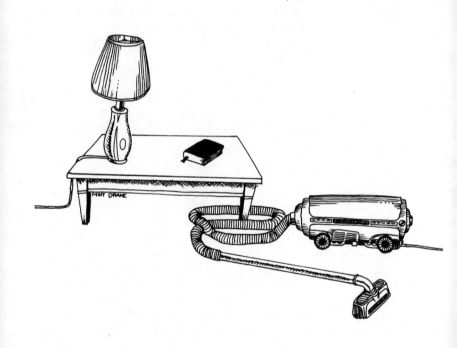

4 / *Bible*

"She rises while yet it is night and gets spiritual food for her household. . . ."[4]

The Wednesday morning Bible study started without me. The outer door announced my arrival as a local wind slammed it shut. The pastor must have heard it too because almost immediately he said, "Amen."

Taking a deep breath, I walked into the church lounge.

"Welcome aboard!" exclaimed the tall, lean pastor who handed me an attendance sheet to sign. His broad smile covered my embarrassment when I caught my toe on one of those metal folding chair legs that stick out so far, and fell into the seat.

"Thank you," I answered softly. I wrote my name down at the bottom of the page and waited. Although my ankle stung, eager anticipation swept over me as I looked around the room. Sunshine poured through the cozy drapes. "Jesus Loves Me" posters graced the walls. And the other members of the group looked friendly enough. I relaxed. *Thus begins beautiful me*, I thought serenely. If I had only known . . .

Enthusiastically, I searched the faces of the other women. I mused about their motivation. Why did they come to Bible study? I knew, of course, why I had come. I wanted to be like Her, and so far strawberries and sewing hadn't done the trick.

Since the pastor had forgotten his notes and had raced two steps at a time over to his study to retrieve them, I reasoned it was as good a time as any to ask the lady sitting next to me if she had ever heard of Her. I meditated for a moment as to how to open the subject. *Have you ever heard of Her?* Too trite—almost insane. *Say, what do you think of the woman in Proverbs 31?* I decided on the direct approach.

Glancing casually past my left elbow, I spoke. "Nice day."

She hadn't heard, since she was busy talking with a woman on her left.

"Ahem!" I cleared my throat.

"Yes?" she queried. Curly white hair framed her face, and her blue eyes twinkled from behind silver-rimmed spectacles. "Do you need a Bible?" Her smile warmed my soul.

I bobbed my head up and down and accepted the slightly musty smelling Bible. "Nice day," I offered.

"Yes," she replied amiably.

I didn't ask. I couldn't! Now cowardice adorned my list of failures.

I settled back in my chair and waited.

"Well, folks," announced the returning minister, "now we can begin!" His cheerful spirit lifted my sagging one, and before I knew it, my first Bible study was over.

Actually I spent more time that morning studying the people at the study than the study itself. It was appalling how I judged each one of their Christian lives by their faces. If a lady had a sour face, I didn't assume her arthritis was killing her. I reasoned that she was unhappy in her Christian experience. It's terrible how quickly judgment falls.

I had arrived at Bible study with one purpose: to get spiritual and be like Her. That's the only reason I gave up my blouse and replaced it with a Bible. I came away wondering how long it would take.

"Good-bye, good-bye," I waved as I walked to my car.

Starting the engine, I puzzled over whether or not I showed some spirituality.

Roaring home at top speed, I said to the car steering wheel, "Good thing nobody's coming home for lunch. It's half past twelve."

Tired, I trudged up the basement stairs which led to the

kitchen. I walked over to the kitchen table and deposited my Bible-study Bible (they said I could keep it), a new notebook, and part of the picket fence which had fallen over again.

"Stupid piece of plastic junk," I muttered. "What I need is a bacon, lettuce and tomato sandwich loaded with mayonnaise and contained in three pieces of crisp toast."

Discouragement over my new venture overcame my anticipation of a BLT. A gloomy voice whispered, "The Bible can be pretty dull, you know. What do you have in common with those women? Why not try something else?"

What? My wandering mind was curious.

"Look here," the suggestion came lilting through, "why not just dig out the blouse with one collar, two sleeves, and a few oil stains, and conquer it?"

I followed that line of reasoning until the oil stains.

I was feeling frustrated and fat. I reasoned that She probably had no difficulty keeping Her weight under control, and I did. My breakfast had been only water—zero calories. Then came the BLT with lots of mayonnaise . . .

Wouldn't you know that our morning scripture dealt with food? "I have not gone back from the commandment of His lips; I have esteemed and treasured up the words of His mouth more than my necessary food."[5]

Ripped asunder by conflict, I poured myself a cup of lukewarm coffee and proceeded toward the large living room window to have a little conversation with the Chief.

The sight of my favorite boulder bathed in sunlight took my breath away. Confidence replaced confusion. Philosophy flooded my brain and my words of wisdom diffused through the plate glass and bombarded the snoozing monolith. "It shouldn't be so difficult to get spiritual, should it?"

The Chief continued his sightless, soundless gazing heavenward.

"I mean," I continued with more vigor, "all I have to do is *discipline* myself in spiritual matters and I cannot fail."

I remembered learning in school that George Washington, the first President of the United States, had said something about discipline being the "soul of an army"; therefore all I had to do was form an army of one (me) and begin advancing upon Her.

The mists of a low rain cloud bumped into the Chief's third feather—it might have been the second—just as I drew my final conclusion and spoke to my giant friend. "Virtue will be mine, Chief. Determination and discipline cannot fail."

Sextus Propertius had said it first in about 25 B.C., "What though strength fails? Boldness is certain to win praise. In mighty enterprises, it is enough to have had the determination." Translated, that says: "Quod si deficiant vires, audacia certe/Laus erit: in magnis et coluisse sat est."

Pleasant as conversing with Chief Rocky-Face was, I remembered I'd been given an assignment to do for next week's Bible study.

Determinedly I faced the task. Pushing aside the piece of picket fence, I opened my new notebook and the Bible.

"Oooops, better find something to write with," I said, jumping up out of the chair just as I got settled.

"There is not a single pen in this house!" I voiced with a certain amount of irritation after fifteen minutes of a "search and retrieve" mission. No matter where I looked—in drawers (mostly screws and bits of plastic), under things (mostly paper), and on top of surfaces (all dust)—my investigation turned up nothing but a half-chewed yellow pencil with the eraser already demolished.

The dust disturbed me to the point of grabbing a dustcloth. Naturally that led me to the vacuum cleaner. SHE rankled my thoughts as I ran around the house throwing dirt out the windows via the dustcloth, and saving squalor in the vacuum bag. "Probably no dust where She lives anyway," I grumped.

Next thing I knew it was Wednesday morning again. The Bible lay unopened, unread, and unnoticed.

"How can this be Wednesday?" I asked the family at breakfast.

They replied by munching toast, gulping coffee, and saying good-bye.

As soon as they were gone, I heaped the breakfast mess on the kitchen counter to be dealt with later, and proceeded to the untouched Bible and lesson. Frantically I read and wrote. "How could a whole week have sailed past without getting my Bible study lesson done?" I groaned and rubbed my nose with my wrist.

Don't ask, my brain advised.

I arrived at Bible study late, but prepared.

Another seven days took wing, and I found myself repeating, "How can this be Wednesday?" to a full laundry basket.

By the third week I was cheating on my homework by asking God for help. "Lord, could you help me get a handle on the Sermon on the Mount?"

Cheating became a habit; and, though I wasn't proud of it, the practice continued. (The reason I felt ashamed of myself was that the preacher kept telling me what a blessing I would receive for all my hard work. I was a little scared of what I was going to receive from God because it didn't seem to me that I should get supernatural help and then claim it as my own work.)

At that point a strange change took place. My lesson assignments were completed on time, the answers were correct, and I began to enjoy the Bible study. Some nodded their heads in various shades of approval as I eagerly shared what God had communicated to me in my moments of helpless panic. I knew I would have to come clean about my source of information and resolved to do it the very next Wednesday.

I drove slowly to the church. The day had arrived.

Nervousness ran up and down my neck like a spider as I dragged myself out of the car and up to the entrance of the church annex. Carefully I opened the heavy outer door, hung on for dear life in case a gust of wind slammed it shut with a loud crash, stepped inside and clicked the door shut.

Laughter, piano playing, and a soprano voice belting out "Onward Christian Soldiers" informed me that something was amiss. Where was the pastor?

A blast of cold air behind me heralded the now-open door.

"Well, hello!" My missing minister exclaimed as the heavy door shot shut. "Looking for me?" His crooked tie and mussed up hair told us he was *late.*

Before I had time to confess, the sleepy-eyed clergyman said,

"I slept in this morning, left my notes at home, and then I couldn't find the car keys."

"That's all right," I exclaimed in a rush, "I've been cheating on my homework for weeks." He looked surprised, but in the clamor of getting started did not respond one way or another.

Confession really is good for the soul, I decided. After my cleansing and renewal, I entered into our Bible study with less determination and more vigor.

The following week the neighbor's cat bit me. The enormous black feline was to be my charge for seven days. He lasted *one*. While entertaining the little lion in my basement, he suddenly jumped in the middle of my back and hung on. That didn't worry me (my neighbor said he liked to do that to her when she hung out the clothes). But later when I picked him up to cuddle him, he sank his fangs into my right hand up to his gums. I didn't die from the bite, but nearly did from the doctor's tetanus shot.

I was thankful I'd already confessed my cheating because the previous evening, when I had had five extra children for supper, the dishwasher short-circuited at the wall socket. Flames leaped, children screamed, and I noticed a nasty leak in the ceiling just above the table. If I hadn't known God wasn't mad at me, I would have been certain that He was pouring out judgment on me.

All of which is to say that on that next Wednesday morning when a new person arrived at our Bible study, I was not smiling. I noticed her looking at me out of the corner of her left eye, but I didn't stop to think until later that she probably wondered if I was happy in my Christian experience.

Finally I began to grasp the significance of studying the Bible with others, and God seemed to have come to terms with my cheating. Nine weeks had passed since that first fearful morning when I'd approached the church lounge. As the study drew to a close, I felt as though I would lose a close friend I'd come to depend upon for strength and comfort.

The Bible study class had taught me something about "busy-ness." This housewife and mother—"homemaker" in the 20th-century term—had been revolving around a fixed point with no direction. This busyness had controlled much of my time and left me feeling frustrated and tired. Before my leap into spirituality, I was "too busy" for the Bible. As days progressed, I found the Bible gave me time and a sense of my destiny.

The Bible began to change me, and eternal questions hung in my mind. But everything fell apart for me again during our last class. While pondering the meaning of my existence, I heard, ". . . *sewing.*"

Sewing? I tuned in both ears, ". . . clothing the lilies of the field; then why doesn't God do things like that today?"

I whipped my head to the right to hear the pastor's response.

"What do you mean?" The minister waited.

Flushing, the speaker continued, "I'm supposed to be seeking the kingdom of God, and that takes time, right?"

Right! My mind agreed.

"Then who does my sewing?" she finished.

"Who does your sewing?"

"Yeah," I chimed in, "who does her sewing?"

"You too?" queried the pastor, turning to me.

Wrinkling up his nose to push up his eyeglasses, he addressed the class, "Anyone else bothered about *sewing*?"

An invigorating discussion followed. Comments flew like grasshoppers across a warm summer hayfield. I could see her point. If it took her as long to sew as it took me to cut out my blouse, her children would be running naked in the streets. However, I understood the pastor's view too. He didn't sew.

Guilt crept along my shoulders as I remembered my unfinished blouse, and I lost my grip. If there were any good conclusions to the discussion, they never penetrated my panic-stricken mental state.

As days sprinted past, I couldn't get it together. My youngest son's birthday approached, and somehow I still owed the middle son a birthday cake from his previous birthday because I hadn't had time. How could I "seek the kingdom" while running behind?

That last Bible study had opened a new can of worms for me. The "Sermon on the Mount" dealt with God's love for us and our love for others. For at least one lady there, sewing for her family was part of her loving them.

And for me? Conflict rose to a dangerous point as I tried to seek God's kingdom first without ignoring my family.

The "sewing" discussion had triggered something inside that pricked at me. I knew the half-finished blouse lurked hidden in the drawer of my dresser. What did I do with my time?

Questions crunched through my mind. Looking back into Proverbs, I realized that She probably didn't have to get spiritual because she already was.

But how did *She* do it?

I could never be like Her.

What was wrong with me? Why was it so important? I knew God wasn't mad at me, but why did His loving me seem to make me miserable?

I felt a dream attack coming on. Perspiration formed along my hairline, and my stomach churned.

Like a lost baby, I cried.

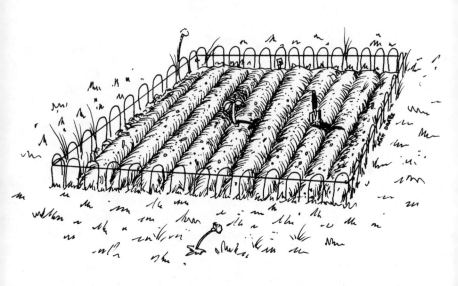

5 / Lost

"A capable, intelligent and virtuous woman, who is he who can find her? She is far more precious than jewels, and her value is far above rubies or pearls."[6]

I sat crumpled in my creaky rocking chair trying to read my dictionary. "Lost," I read through the blur, ". . . having wandered from, or unable to find, the way as a *lost* sheep. . . ."

Another tear trickled down my left cheek as I rocked back and forth, listening to the familiar "squeak, swak" of the old rocker. I rubbed my finger over the marks on the left arm of the chair where my middle son had cut his first two teeth. *What's wrong with me?*

The clock on the wall answered, "Cuckoo!"

"No, I'm not cuckoo. I'm miserable," I responded to the idiot bird who had disappeared into his clock.

I should have been happy. My plants, all lined up along the large living room window, were growing by leaps and bounds. No longer seeds, they were sprouts basking in the warmth of sunshine which streamed through the window. The tiny leaves strained toward the solar energy.

Self-pity, that terrible state that focuses on self, had me in its awful tentacles. For that moment I felt as if I were the only one in all the world who felt pain.

It seemed almost identical to the time when my father had momentarily lost me in a large department store. The terror and

49

suffering I endured seemed like forever until I heard my name and ran as fast as I could to the sound of his voice.

Other times of feeling alone flashed before my mind's eye—walking down the aisle as a bride, the labor room at my first son's birth, graduation from college.

Rocking by myself in the sun-bathed living room, I wondered if other women ever felt that way. Was I the only one? These events did share one common factor—beginnings. Were all beginnings marked with pain? I wondered.

It had to be true, I reasoned. Beginnings hurt.

Beginning anything causes pain because change hurts. The human condition finds alterations—dieting, exercise, advanced schooling—difficult. People would rather perish than have to change their direction. If I'd known much then about the Spirit of God, I would have realized that a pearl of great price forms out of irritation to an oyster. And that dissatisfaction with one's self often precedes growth in the Christian life.

But I knew nothing of how that ancient lady became Her. She seemed to develop naturally, effortlessly.

Little really mattered at that moment because I was busy reflecting on a green pea seed I'd planted in the garden that morning. I always felt bad when I put the crinkly white seed into the finger-sized hole in the ground. It must have been quite cold and dark, and I could just imagine the hideous wait to sprout.

Carrot seeds, though, gave me no such pause. They seemed to nestle close together while lining themselves in a furrow of dirt. The green pea seed, however, reminded me of a burial.

Depression usually didn't trouble me, and, in spite of myself, my mood lifted from melancholy to pensive pondering.

"I am no longer nineteen," I sighed as I rose from the chair and approached the living room window to view the Chief. "I'm aging, Chief." I spoke softly.

What's that got to do with planting seeds? My mind filled in for Old Boulder Face.

"Listen, Chief. I could find twenty new gray hairs if I tried, and wrinkles, and aging spots. . . ."

I decided not to look in the mirror.

Real beauty, I'd learned in a recent Bible study, develops on the inside and shines through to overcome the aging process. Had I begun my inner growth in time?

What did my family see in me? Did they see a tiny green shoot forcing its way upward through the soil to the sun? Or did they see a burial?

I sighed. People hardly ever notice the inner workings of other humans. The effort involved hides the advantage of discovery.

"Maybe that's why people stay so busy," I announced, straightening my shoulders at the thought.

"Yes." The answer seemed to come from somewhere deep inside.

The Chief continued his vigil as I spoke to his granite face. "When I'm really occupied, Chief," I squinted into the sun, "I fail to notice time ticking away. After all, the ebb tide leads to death. Who wants to cope with mortality before it's necessary?"

"I am the Resurrection and the Life," the quiet assurance rose to my consciousness.

Truth: Busyness is a cover-up for the pain of reality. When death walks near, or tragedy strikes, we get busy.

Grabbing my Bible from the coffee table, I sank back into the old rocker and looked up "lost" in the concordance at the back.

Running my finger down the columns of references, I found, "I will seek the lost. . . ."[7]

Goose bumps of awe popped up on my arms as I read about God looking for the lost and retrieving the scattered. Rocking furiously, I grappled with the thought.

I'm like a little seed. Only I'm not really buried to God. I'm just waiting to be found. All I have to do is wait and I will grow.

Hope placed her gentle touch upon my soul and swept away the lost and lonely feelings. Bouncing out of the rocker, I joined my plants in the sunshine which streamed into the living room and formed a bright rectangle on the carpet.

"I'm okay now, Chief," I assured him briefly before turning my back and heading into the kitchen.

I cheerfully scrubbed away at the skillet caked with dried scrambled eggs. I hardly minded the boiled-over coffee stains on the stove top, or the ketchup just above the sink. Whisking away the red globs, I realized that although Bible study was finished, I had just begun. Hope! Hope lifted me up above the leaking dishwasher, the cold water faucet that wouldn't quit dripping, and the new chip on the refrigerator door.

Jesus doesn't see me the way I am, I thought, *but the way I will be!*

Wiping my hands and putting away the dish towel, I said a small prayer, "Help me look at you, Lord, and be glad."

Peace filled my heart as I waltzed through the laundry. I even kissed the dog on top of her head, instead of kicking her off the couch as I usually did. She looked mystified but grateful.

"I think I'll do some grocery shopping for the family," I happily announced to Ben, the guinea pig. He squealed his reply. He thought I was "gonna get him a carrot."

However, my light heart gave rise to a creative list of luxurious food to purchase and menus to feed an army for the next two weeks. It was wonderful.

I charged downtown to the supermarket singing "Onward Christian Soldiers" all the way. I even cheered something like, "Go, God, Go!" It didn't seem disrespectful. It was a carryover from my days as a high school cheerleader. God and I were a team.

Pride went before me—and the fall.

It didn't seem like pride. More like innocence. I'm not certain at what point I elbowed the Lord out of the way and took over myself, but God's part of the team would not have done what I did at the supermarket.

But the Lord was not dissuaded by my efforts to show Him how good I was and how others might improve. God needed to show me a little of my real self.

It could be put off no longer. When I entered the supermarket, I turned into a monster. I use the word "monster" advisedly because only a beast of greed could do what I did.

Frying chickens were on sale at a remarkably low price. I'm not sure what happened to me—I don't think I blacked out—but I went absolutely *wild* at the chicken counter. In almost one scoop, I popped thirteen chickens into my basket.

I peddled my basket as fast as I could to the bacon section.

Almost a dollar less per pound than usual! My eyes glazed over at the pink, meaty packages stacked neatly before me. I helped myself!

There stood Bible-study-me facing the world, the flesh, and the devil. I lost on all three counts. My grocery cart filled to the brim, I struggled to push the heavy load to the check-out lane.

Here is the worst part. I didn't realize my sin of greed. I felt righteous. I was saving money for my husband, wasn't I?

The Lord wasn't the only one who saw me. Just outside the store, a Bible-study friend spoke to me about my behavior. "You filled your basket with chickens so fast I feared you would break it! I felt like tackling a chicken on the way by just to hand to the lady who waited so patiently behind you."

"I didn't see you or the lady behind me!" I exclaimed, bewildered. "Do you think anyone else saw?" Perspiration formed along my hairline, I rubbed my nose with my wrist, and quickly smoothed my eyebrows with my index finger.

"Well," she responded, "they might have missed the chicken episode, but I doubt they missed your performance at the bacon counter."

My knees began to buckle. I clutched at the cart handle. "What did I do there?" I inquired in a very small voice.

"It couldn't go unnoticed that you took the best ten pounds of bacon with one swipe of your hand—"

"Please, no more," I groaned.

"—but your elbows were flying everywhere so fast that nobody else could get near the counter—not even the store clerk who wanted to replenish the supply."

Driving home, the shock hit me. Horrified, I pulled into the driveway and stopped. The trunk was filled with my ill-gotten gain, and my heart was heavy with my terrible Christian example and my gross greed. How could I have done it? I'd just finished promising myself that I would be sensitive to others.

At least I'd remembered to thank my Bible-study friend for her bravery in sharing what she had witnessed. Small compensation.

Slowly, shoulders sagging with a sore spirit, I trudged the

heavy pork and fowl into the basement and packed the spoil into the deep freeze.

Climbing the stairs leading up to the kitchen, I pulled myself along, weighted down by my guilt and failure. The rocker beckoned me.

As I lowered myself into the chair, I envisioned Her giving away chickens from her own grocery cart to everyone who passed.

Grabbing the vacuum cleaner, I determined that cleanliness was next to godliness. During the next three weeks, I struggled with my behavior while vacuuming and scrubbing anything in the house that merely threatened to look dusty. I was a human being; therefore, I would make mistakes. I'd learned in Bible study that God would forgive my mistakes if I repented. As humbly as I could, I turned away from greed. Each time I served a chicken or prepared bacon, I remembered . . . and was sad.

While remorse didn't help me, my changed attitude allowed the God who loved me to do some changing from within. In retrospect I could see that my performance in greed—the supermarket scene—was only the tip of the iceberg of wanting the best for myself. That frightened me.

What encouraged me to continue was the sense of peace which followed my sincere apology to God for what I'd done.

I began to understand that part of God's gigantic love is His capacity to accept us just as we are. If I would be willing to see, a bit at a time, the rest of my iceberg of sin, then God would melt that frozen mountain and hard heart into pools of warm righteousness.

Me? Righteous? I chuckled out loud at the thought.

The spring sunshine wrapped my shoulders as I sat in my rocking chair reading my Bible. "For the Son of Man has come to seek and to save that which was lost."[8]

I'd heard the call of Jesus Christ just as surely as I'd responded to my father's voice when I was little and lost in the large department store. Found! I'd laughed through my tears when I had seen my daddy coming to take me home.

Found. By the Heavenly Father. Safe in His love until He took me home. Rocking slowly, I thought about the tiny green pea seed again. It was probably happy waiting under the soil.

Did it know it would become a lush, green plant with delicate white flowers, that it would bear tender green peas?

Could a green pea seed see into the future? Could I?

For the seed, God provided sunshine and water. For me, He supplied the love of His Son, the truth of His Word, and the strength of His Spirit.

Suddenly I heard the clamor of voices.

"Mom, didya get the hamster bedding yet? Hampst can't stand sleeping on the cold floor of his cage."

"Mom, why are you in that chair? Are you sick?"

"What's for supper, Mom?"

Smiling at each one in turn, I answered gently, "I'm germinating."

"Oh," they responded in unison and departed to their rooms.

The battle had just begun.

SUMMER

6 / *Beachhead*

"She extends her hand to the poor; and she stretches out her hands to the needy."[9]

Oh, what a beautiful morning . . . Oh, what a beautiful beach . . .
I hummed to myself as my eyes scanned the lakeshore for likely people to help. Squinting against the bright sunlight, I grabbed my shades for a better view and leaned back in the chaise lounge.

What a happy discovery! While searching the lakeside crowd for a needy person, I spied my husband, my big, huge angel, and my three stair-step sons. They created a perfect picture of summer.

The two biggest boys were playing ball with their dad in the center of shimmering water. George, the youngest, was snorkeling along the edge of the lake where it was barely a foot deep. Wearing his head gear and flippers, he looked like a gigantic insect. *Probably trying to discover a way to tunnel to the center of the earth*, I reasoned peacefully.

Since hubby had everything under control, I welcomed the chance to close my eyes and recall the events leading up to this moment—me lying on a sunny beach.

I'd come a long way since the day I sat feeling lost and alone in the old rocker, not wanting to see the light of day. Germinating had led to sprouting, and soon I was off and running with my new-found life in Jesus. (I should have noticed that my plants didn't pull out their roots and run around the garden, but I didn't.)

Anyway, as the days of spring slipped into the heat of summer, I read my Bible with renewed vigor and determination. That is, I determined to put into practice what the Bible said. I reasoned that was how She did it. "If She can, so can I!"

Obviously, She helped the poor and needy. It stated that in Proverbs. I also would aid the impoverished and the destitute, and so become more like Her. It was a plan that could not fail. Hadn't I read in Jeremiah, "They cannot harm you. . . . For I am with you. . . . I will deliver you"?[10]

Success wouldn't escape me this time. I formed a plan of action. "I must reach out!" I stated emphatically.

Since my mate wasn't teaching school in the summer, I schemed to take care of two birds with one trip. Not only could we enjoy the beach, I could reach out my hands to those on the sand. . . .

After making my dear spouse his favorite chocolate chip cookies, I approached the subject of spending a few days camping at a nearby lake.

"Like the cookies, dear?" I smiled as sweetly as I knew how while pouring him a steaming cup of coffee.

"Ummm, great. What's the catch?" He grabbed two more cookies off the plate.

"Catch? How can you say a thing like that, honey?"

"You want to spend a few days at the lake, right?" He chomped another tasty morsel, wiped his fingers on the linen napkin I'd provided, and sipped the hot coffee.

"Right," I admitted. "But how did you know?"

"A little bird told me," he replied, grinning.

I threw him another cookie which landed exactly where I aimed it—his left shoulder.

"Missed my mouth!" he teased. "Get packing. We'll do it."

And that's how I found myself bumping along a winding dirt road listening to the kids sing, "Over the hills and through the bumps to Gloria Lake we go."

"Hurry, Dad!" yelled the youngest.

"Go for it, Dad," came the deepening voice of John Jr.

"Yawn, sigh," commented the middle son.

"How much farther?" I asked, anxious to get on with my mission.

"Here's the parking lot now," my husband answered us collectively and turned into a paved area.

As soon as he pulled over and stopped, the boys leaped out and began to pack our belongings on their backs. We didn't want to make more than one trip down to the beach.

"We'll find a campsite later," my thoughtful spouse suggested.

"Fine," I responded. I was just as eager as the boys to get to the lake, but for another reason.

It was amazing how much gear we carried—one gallon of water, two gallons of tea mixed with fruit juice, fried chicken, four air mattresses, two blankets, one chaise lounge, a beach ball, a hamper full of marshmallows and cookies, two backpacks containing beach towels, extra clothing, squirt guns, winter jackets, and a scuba diving set.

The winter jackets probably weren't necessary, but I wanted to be prepared for any emergency.

We dropped a few things on the way to the shore, but the trail we left behind was easy to spot. The boys energetically raced back and retrieved our things.

Quickly I'd scanned the beach looking for a poor, needy person to help.

"Can we go swimming now, Mom?" George smiled into my eyes with all the charm he could muster.

"Ask your father," I replied, half hearing him.

Next thing I knew, they were in the water, and I was in the chaise lounge.

"Want to go swimming, Mom?" Icy water dripped on my hot skin and jolted me back to the present.

Opening my eyes, I responded evenly, "Not now, kids. I'm busy. A little later, okay?"

"Okay," they chorused. "Dad said to ask you because we want you to have a good time too," and they raced back to the water.

Their yellow bathing suits flashed across the white sand like a comet streaking across the night sky as they raced back to the water. I waved happily to my husband.

Settling down into my chaise lounge, I prepared to begin my assault on the beach. I envisioned my chair as my base of operations, and my objective: a poor and needy person. My heart beat faster in anticipation. She would never match this!

Shading my eyes with my hands, I looked around. I didn't want to seem too conspicuous. *Oh, no!* I thought. *How am I going to tell what a poor and needy person looks like?*

My heart sank as I peered around the area. Many people filled the beach, but they all wore bathing suits. *I'm not going to recognize a poor and needy person by a bathing suit,* I reasoned—*there's no room for patches.*

I didn't see even a lonely person. Everybody seemed to have at least one companion.

Strike one! My mind shouted.

Then I saw him. Just about two blankets away a young fellow slept on the sand. "Why, he doesn't even have a blanket!" I exclaimed. "Maybe he's my lost and needy person to save," I muttered zealously while sitting upright in my chair. I watched him carefully as he slumbered, and tried to gather my courage to approach him, wake him up, and extend friendly greetings.

Finally I stood up and began walking toward him.

Imagine my chagrin when four bathing beauties beat me to it and surrounded him with blankets. He wasn't alone either.

Strike two! yelled my brain.

Putting a towel over my face, I lay back in the chaise lounge. *How could that have happened?* Quickly I reviewed the facts. *I came here to find and save a lost and needy person, or to help a poor one, and I can't even recognize one.* I felt incredibly embarrassed.

Deciding to ignore the failure of that small skirmish, I allowed the sun to bathe away my humiliation. The warmth felt good beating down on my tender skin, and my mind meandered over other subjects, including the deep, dark tan which would soon be mine. I closed my eyes. . . .

"And does not eat the bread of idleness."[11] Her voice had a hint of laughter in it.

I bolted upright in my chair so fast I tipped over into the

sand. Peals of laughter rang out for real. "Were you the one snickering?" I instantly recognized the face of my middle son, Joe, gawking at me.

"All right. Now you're going to get it!" I grabbed one of the air mattresses and slugged him with it.

"Help! Help!" He screeched at the top of his lungs. Before I could swing at him again, reinforcements arrived in the form of a flippered snorkle wearer and an almost six-foot son carrying a pail of lake water.

"Get her! Get her!" The troops shouted.

Oblivious to the sleeping sunbathers around us, we swash-buckled the air, hitting madly at each other and missing most of the time. Next came the water attack. Two squirt guns fired and didn't miss. The full pail of lake water, hurled by my oldest son, hit me square in the head and soaked my freshly permed hair.

"Yeeeeaaaah!" I shrieked, and snatched the gallon jug of ice water from home. "You'll pay for that!" I shouted at all three of them.

Making the greatest throw of my life, I missed the kids and hit the people on my left. To make matters worse, the jug slipped out of my hands and landed in the middle of a lady's sandwich.

Strike three, and you're out! my subconscious commented.

"Hook shot!" howled Joe, jumping up and down with glee.

Before I could get the boys settled down, the beach began to clear. "Too bad Dad wasn't here to join in the fun," laughed young George in his innocence.

"Where is your father anyway?" I queried, relieved that he hadn't seen me in action.

"He went for a walk. I think he was talking about town business to somebody," answered my baby seriously.

I stood on the beach, my carefully chosen battleground, and took stock of my losses. Watching the boys return to the water, my spirit sagged in frustration. Somehow I'd bitten off more than I could chew. Instead of saving the world, I'd found myself wiped out. The enemy hadn't needed to *offer* me an apple to bite.

Instead of advancing and securing even one person who might have needed anything, I'd landed on a hostile shore secured and defended by an advance force. The enemy of my soul, the one who had tempted Eve and tormented Jesus, tripped me up and I fell.

"Where did I go wrong?" I asked myself, since no one else remained near me. "I've made a fool of myself," I continued, "and worst of all She wouldn't have done what I did."

I sat in the chaise lounge feeling sorry for myself and watching the sun sink lower into the sky. The boys were almost blue, and I was baked lobster red by the time my husband returned from his walk. My humor matched my skin.

"Sleeping, hon?" inquired my mate.

"I want to go home," I spoke shortly.

"You what?" He asked in amazement.

"I said, 'I want to go home.' " I retorted.

Rolling his eyes heavenward, he knew better than to say much more, but I could see the disappointment in his face, and I didn't care. Misery loves company, and I wanted companionship, not reason.

Somehow he explained to the boys that I wasn't feeling well again, and they all loaded the car while I sat in my chaise lounge.

"It's all Her fault," I justified my actions to myself while folding up the chair and following their trail to the car.

"You sure?" he questioned one more time before starting the motor.

"I'm positive," I said in a monotone voice.

Driving home, I stared out the window. Instead of reaching out to the poor and stretching out my hands to the needy, I'd left a wake of destruction. To me, the sands represented a beachhead—an area to secure and conquer for God; a place to give away some of what had been given to me.

What a flop! I thought in despair.

"Tired?" My husband's voice was full of loving concern.

"Yes, I guess I am," I replied. I was weary all right, but not with the type of fatigue that could be remedied by sleep. And on top of my other failures, I hated myself for ruining the family outing.

"How 'bout you?" A wave of emotion swept over me as I turned my head and glanced at my husband at the wheel. It was a mixture of deep warmth, gratitude, and loneliness all wrapped into one quick feeling.

"I'm fine," he answered and reached over to pat my hand. We held hands the rest of the way home, and I wished with all my heart that peace would come back to my soul.

Nobody said much as he and the boys unloaded the car, refrigerated the perishable food, and neatly put away the camping gear.

Total misery engulfed me as I retreated to the bathtub to rinse away the sand and wash my hair. The rest of the family was asleep, when sitting alone in my rocking chair, I wept tears of frustration and anger.

"Mom?" I heard the hushed voice of John Jr. and the creaking floor boards as he approached me in the living room. "I can't sleep. Are you okay?"

Hastily I brushed away the telltale tears and smiled, "I'm fine, sweetie," I responded with forced cheerfulness.

"Good." He came around in front of me. "I was thirsty, so I thought I'd have a glass of milk," he explained.

Looking up at his face reddened by the bright summer sun, his serious eyes, and his mussed-up blond hair, I commented, "We're going to have two men around here pretty soon." After pausing, I blurted, "I'm sorry about the beach."

"That's okay," he replied with the same loving concern shown earlier by his father; "it's supposed to rain anyway."

After a couple of glasses of milk, he returned to bed, and I continued to rock thoughtfully to and fro. *What a mixture he is*, I mused; *one minute he's a man and the next moment he's my little son.* But I didn't see the connection between his physical growth and my spiritual development for a long time.

Meanwhile, still striving to be like Her, I continued to reach out to the "poor and needy," creating a stir wherever I landed. It didn't dawn on me that I couldn't help anyone else until I knew what I was doing. Marshalling my energies on beachhead after beachhead, I wiped out in battle, but I refused to give up the war.

She was getting to me again. I felt myself slipping. It wasn't anything I could put my finger on, but I seemed to be busy, busier, busiest, but dissatisfied. My dream attacks occurred more frequently, and I couldn't catch hold of the peace that had reigned at our house for a while. Instead, frustration ruled me with an iron hand.

Something was wrong, but what?

The next Sunday morning I found a clue.

Arriving late to the service (which my patient spouse detested), I was thankful that the congregation was still singing the opening hymn. It was indeed a blessing that the people stood to sing; coming in the side door, we threaded our way through pews and people to get to the back only to discover that all the chairs were filled. We had to parade back up to the very front row. We filled the first pew just as everyone sang, "Aaaaaa-mehhn."

Breathing a sigh of relief, I was grateful that at least I'd cut the boys' hair, fixed a hearty breakfast, and hemmed my new dress. I noted also with pride my husband's freshly ironed shirt (no scorches), and the cleanly scrubbed faces of the two youngest sons, and only one small cut on John Jr. where he practiced his new shaving technique.

My new dress must have impressed the lady behind me because she tapped on my shoulder just before the offering. I could hardly wait for the compliment to follow and I turned around quickly.

"The tag on your dress is hanging out," she whispered.

"What?" I hissed back.

"The tag—the price tag. Here, I'll fix it for you." Whereupon she stuffed the sharp paper tag down in under the collar where it scratched at me for the remainder of the service.

As I said, a clue offered itself, but an answer eluded me.

While people I tried to save felt sorry for me, it led me to conclude that I was no closer to my goal of becoming like Her than I was to start with. (One positive note, however: I caused laughter wherever I went.)

The clue I mentioned wafted into my head as I sat squirming under the price tag during the sermon. Somehow, the minister's voice faded out as an idea floated into my mind. The suggestion was so strong it blotted out his words of wisdom.

I'm going about this all wrong, I concluded.

Sitting there wriggling my neck to avoid poking at the annoying tag with my hand, I recalled a few war facts I'd learned in school.

1. Good soldiers, when losing a battle, change tactics, using a new strategy when necessary.

2. The winning team succeeds by using a good offense as its defense.

3. Trickiness helps (or words to that effect).

By the time the preacher pronounced the benediction, I had the perfect plan. I would organize myself. Orderly opposition would neutralize Her and bring sweet victory to me.

After church my family sat in amazement while I served them crisp fried chicken with lots of gravy to pour on creamy whipped potatoes, steaming corn on the cob (no limit on butter), and their favorite hot rolls. I proudly presented them with a cake fresh from the oven—devil's food, smothered in thick chocolate fudge frosting.

"What's this?" asked my suspicious spouse.

"Counterattack," I sweetly replied.

Underneath my saintly expression lurked do-or-die determination.

I didn't bother to consult my Bible or God the next morning before I unveiled my plan of action to the Chief.

"You see, my granite-headed friend, I am sick of making a fool out of myself by trying to copy Her behavior. I wind up looking like a complete moron, totally out of my mind. I figure a few military tactics of order and discipline borrowed from the great commanders of the past and a little of the world's wisdom should fix things nicely."

As usual, he stared sightless into the great beyond.

"So, Chief, I think it's time you and I get some organization going around here! Don't you agree?"

The witless wonder continued his mute vigil.

I didn't understand that being a fool for Christ was better than becoming worldly wise.

I was about to learn.

7 / *Organization*

"She looks well to how things go in her household. . . ."[12]

As I sat holding my foot in a basin of steaming water, I wondered if She had ever suffered from an ingrown toenail.

"This is definitely going to slow me down," I moaned out loud to an empty bathtub. The night before I'd tried soaking my big toe in a kettle of very hot water in the living room while watching television. I knocked the pot over in a fit of excitement over the movie, and the scalding liquid burned my other foot. Excruciating pain in the sore toe and moderate discomfort from the other burned foot brought me to my knees to ask the Lord for help. Getting organized without mobility was going to be difficult even with my present determination. So I asked God if He would see fit to fix it.

I shouldn't have asked.

As soon as I'd finished boiling and praying, I hobbled around the house to see what needed to be done. Recalling that fine Sunday morning when I had devised my orderly plan of attack, I decided that cleaning the house would be the first item on my agenda.

When I had checked Her out in Proverbs, I'd discovered that She kept her house tidy. "Saturday is a perfect day to begin," I had announced to the boys, who all of a sudden had places to go. "I'll wait," I cheerfully told them. It had been some wait, but I had more determination than they and had finally won.

So this morning, just as I managed to bump down the basement stairs on the largest part of my anatomy, I heard the boys at the back door.

"Welcome!" I shouted.

"Maybe we should play golf with Dad," suggested George hopefully.

"Forget it," I responded. "You get to play clean-the-deep-freeze with me."

"Look, I'll show you," I said happily to three glum faces as I hopped toward the freezer; "it's full of ice."

Hauling myself up by my arms, I opened the lid and displayed the two and a half inches of frost which had accumulated. "How do you suppose it got like this?" I inquired like a top drill sergeant.

"It worked overtime," piped up Joe.

"For that little bit of sarcasm, you get to clean the most," I shot back. A look of stubbornness crossed his face, and I changed my tone to "gentle."

"Really, guys, it won't be so bad. You'll see." I grinned from ear to ear to demonstrate my good humor.

"But what about your toe, Mom?" George offered.

"My toe will be fine because I'm going to supervise. I promise I won't meddle."

Three blank expressions covered three brains going at a furious rate. But they said nothing.

"Well then," I said smiling, "let's get started."

I sat down on an old kitchen chair and propped my foot up on the seat of another vintage kitchen chair. "First," I ordered, "we unload it. Then we defrost it, and then we load it up again. Isn't that simple?"

Six eyes looked as if they were about to attend an execution. They remained silent because they knew that to try to dissuade me in my state of determination was like trying to halt a moving freight train.

"We'll be through in no time," I encouraged. "Really we will." I hoped my enthusiasm was contagious.

The boys dutifully began hauling meat and bread out of the freezer and loading it into laundry baskets.

When the baskets overflowed, they put the rest of the contents into lawn chairs. Then they trucked boiling water down the stairs and sloshed it into the empty chest. Finally, after soaking up all the excess water and scrubbing the interior, they began to load it up again.

It was at this point that I offered my services. They were looking very tired.

"How 'bout I help a bit, guys? You're looking pretty soggy."

"No, Mom. It's really all right. We're almost finished. See?" They gestured toward the shiny freezer. "Remember your toe. What if you drop a frozen roast on it?"

"Nonsense. I'll be careful. You two older ones go upstairs and start cleaning up the water mess. George and I can handle this quite nicely, can't we?" I stared intently at my youngest.

He nodded affirmatively on cue, "Sure, Mom," but he looked doubtful.

I hobbled over to the freezer and peeked down inside. "Good job, kids!" I encouraged. "Now, Short Stuff, you hand me the meat, and I'll put it in. That way I won't have to walk."

"Okay, Mom," he replied dubiously.

Balancing myself on my hip bones on the edge, I rearranged the food in a tidy fashion. The boys had a habit of just throwing things in, and I wanted to be able to choose a chicken at a moment's notice and not have to dig past a ham to locate it.

Then I came across a stubborn piece of round steak which had attached itself to a frozen frying chicken. I pulled and tugged, but it would not let go.

A chunk of beef stuck to a chicken would thwart my plan of order. I wouldn't have any peace of mind unless I managed to separate the two. I resolved to break them apart by brute force.

Favoring my tender toe, I leaned over a little farther into the freezer to get a better grip. Preparing myself for a mighty yank, I lost my balance and pitched forward so fast all I had time to say was, "Oh, no!" before landing head first inside the freezer.

I heard George giggle before he inquired, "Hey, Mom? Are you coming out?"

"No, I'm not coming out. I am stuck in here, and if you don't do something, I'm going to remain in here and probably freeze to death before suppertime."

At the mention of supper, he chuckled again; "Why don't you pick out something tasty while you're in there?"

"Don't get smart like your brother," I snapped, my tone at a dangerous level.

During the fall, my right arm had lodged itself behind the freezer divider and in between the freezer wall and the frozen chickens. I hated myself for my greedy chicken spree in the supermarket. "Why did I have to buy so many fowl birds?" I moaned as I struggled to get free.

"Is your toe all right?" My youngest inquired.

"My toe is fine. It's up in the air." Using my right shin and my left elbow as a sort of crane. I wrestled around in the freezing cold trying to pry myself loose. The sounds of my tussling alerted my freckle-faced friend to the fact that I really was in trouble.

"Hey, Mom," he manfully announced, "I'll save you!" He grabbed me around the middle and, with strength I did not know he had, pulled me out.

"Owwww!" I shouted as my arm wrenched free of the beef. Falling backwards onto my throbbing toe, I crumpled to the floor like a sack of potatoes.

"Do you want me to get the other guys?" My son showed some genuine concern at last.

I groaned, "No. I'll be fine. Just let me sit here for a moment."

Pulling myself up to a standing position at the edge of the freezer, I managed a smile. "We can finish now. I think we'll just let some of the chickens stick to some of the beef."

Half an hour later I crawled up the stairs and slumped gratefully into the nearest chair and tried to figure out what I had learned from the experience.

I refused to relinquish my stand. The next Saturday that Daddy was playing golf found me standing in front of three worried boys.

"Onward, kids!" I spoke, winsomely holding my Bible. "Look what I just found."

"What?" they replied without really wanting to know.

"She girds herself with strength, and makes her arms strong."[13]

"You're going to lift weights?" from the middle wisecracker.

"No, I'm not going to lift anything. We're going to shampoo the carpets."

"But your toe. . . !" The genuine concern almost weakened my resolve.

"Never mind my toe. It will be fine. It's almost well. Besides, I asked the Lord to fix it, and He will. Now let's get going." And down to the store we went to rent a steam carpet cleaner, so easy to handle that any child could do it. Huffing and puffing, we managed to get it back home, through the garage, and up the stairs into the living room.

"Watch this, Chief," I muttered out the window as I pictured the lovely clean carpet we would have.

The furniture was heavy, but the sewing machine cabinet was impossible. It simply would not move.

"Let's take the drawers out," suggested practical John Jr.

"Let's take the machine out," offered Joe.

"Let's quit," chimed in the last. I had just enough time to catch the glint of braces before my warning stare replaced his look of insurrection to quiet surrender.

"Get going and *pull!*" I commanded. The tallest grabbed one end, and I gripped the part nearest me. Nothing happened.

"What are you doing—pushing or pulling?" I demanded.

"You said to *pull,*" he groaned.

"I meant," I punctuated exasperated puffs, "I pull and *you push.*"

We both gave a mighty heave-ho, and the whole thing fell over on my sore toe.

"You did *what* to your toe?" My darling spouse was incredulous as I lay on the sofa.

"It's going to be all right. The doctor said so. Not only that, dropping the sewing machine on it removed the nail so that I'll never require surgery. . . ."

During my recuperation I began to wonder about the power of prayer. While I was thankful that I wouldn't have to worry about my ingrown toenail anymore, it seemed to me that God had overdone the cure just a bit.

While I was vacuuming the closet in one of the bedrooms one day, a Bible verse popped into my head. Unable to recall it exactly, I found a concordance and looked up the passage.

"Do not be conformed to this world—this age, fashioned after and adapted to its external, superficial customs. But be transformed (changed) by the [entire] renewal of your mind—by its new ideals and its new attitude—so that you may prove [for yourselves] what is the good and acceptable and perfect will of God. . . [in His sight *for you*]."[14]

A quiet voice reminded me, "God is on your side—He wants what is right *for you*. With all your efforts to change, you forget about God's love." I was so elated I raced out of the room to call a friend and share my findings!

I forgot the vacuum which was still in the closet, but no matter. Joe discovered it for me after school, and I managed to respond courteously to his snide remarks about how a grown woman could lose a vacuum cleaner.

"I know God loves me," I told my mountain friend, "and that's all the organization I need."

8 / Skylab

"She fears not the snow for her family, for all her household are doubly clothed in scarlet."[15]

In contrast to Her, I wasn't worried about snow right now since it was summer. I was, however, in a state of panic about what I'd heard was heading for our house.

Remember *Skylab*? The space station the experts put up but forgot to figure out how it must come down?

My husband, who was working on his master's degree, had other topics on his mind. "Don't worry about it," he advised. "If something that big hits you, you won't feel it anyway," he assured me with husbandly calm.

That was fine for him to say, but I felt duty-bound to devise a plan for saving our family—just in case. I listened carefully to the reports of Skylab's progress. I ran from the television to the radio and from network to network in order to ascertain the latest information.

Splash-down (or crash-down) for Skylab was three orbits away. Where would it land? The west coast of North America could be the target. I envisioned California, Oregon, Washington, and British Columbia sinking under the weight of the massive missile.

Mentally I calculated the odds—well, maybe "calculated" is a little strong here, but I was very concerned and doing a lot of frantic planning. Since we lived on the west coast, we were going to get it. The radio announcer had said to take precautions. What safety measures could we take against a mass of gigantic metal?

I opened my Bible to Proverbs—and Her.

"She fears not . . ." That was fine for *Her* to say. She sounded like my husband. ". . . doubly clothed in scarlet," whatever that meant. I closed the Bible.

After pacing the floor, I opened it again. "There has to be an answer in here somewhere," I muttered. Leafing through the pages, I stopped cold at the story of Rahab. Wasn't there something in it about "scarlet"?

Very interesting! "Behold, when we come into the land, you shall bind this scarlet cord in the window through which you let us down, and you shall bring . . . all your . . . household, into your house."[16] A glimmer of an idea began as I read, ". . . and she bound the scarlet cord in the window."[17]

"That's it!" I exclaimed to the cuckoo clock on the living room wall. "There must be something special about *scarlet*. . . ." And I was already grabbing the car keys and heading for my friend Viv at the fabric store.

"Viv, I need something red to make a covering." I was half-way through the sentence before I reached the counter.

"Oh? Are you going to make another blouse, dear?"

Not wanting to admit I hadn't finished the last one after all her help, I hedged, "Not exactly. I was thinking more along the line of curtains."

"Red curtains?" Her eyebrows shot toward her hairline before her composure shoved them back into place. "Of course. Drapes or sheers?"

"I was thinking more like *fast* kitchen curtains?"

"Really. I'm sure you'll do fine," she encouraged me. She was already pursing her lips in concentration and heading toward a section of red fabric. "You won't be needing an expensive fabric then."

"No, the color is more important than style," I replied easily, walking beside her. "I was thinking of cherry red."

"Cherry red," she responded; "—that will be, uh, bright and cheerful. Or how about a cherry red calico?"

"No," I replied confidently, "not a print."

"You're certain?"

"Oh, yes!" I assured her.

We settled on fire engine red broadcloth. "Do you have any scarlet cord?" I inquired.

"I thought you weren't making drapes?" Her quizzical expression creased into a perturbed frown. She eyed me suspiciously.

"Never mind," I flushed. "I—I was just thinking out loud."

She looked at me long and carefully before cutting the fabric. After acquiring enough for plain gathered curtains—Viv had figured the mathematical details of how much I would need—I whipped home as fast as I could drive.

Taking out my recently acquired sewing shears, I made quick work of cutting out four strips of red fabric long enough to cover the kitchen window. "Clothing the window is almost as good as making something red for each family member. Cheaper—more practical," I reasoned as I worked.

"The very lives of my family depend upon my success with this little project," I encouraged myself. It was as easy as one, two, three, and I alternately hummed and whistled while I worked. I didn't even turn on the radio for a report on Skylab until I got the material stitched together.

The kitchen window hangings lay in front of me almost completed. I'd cut each pair the same size for speed of assembly, and I'd decided against sewing a scarlet cord along the bottom. Viv had suggested pompons for trim, but speed was more important than appearances. "They're red, and that's the main part," I comforted myself as I put away the sewing machine, scissors, thread and sewing basket. "I haven't time to hem them," I concluded ruefully, as Skylab's third orbit and supper preparation loomed over me. "I'll just turn them up with masking tape," I decided. The tape hardly showed after they were hung on the rods.

I flipped the radio on for a progress report. Terror gripped me as I heard, ". . . Skylab's plummet to earth . . ."

"What?" I squeaked to the radio.

Just then the sound went to a steady hum. The radio station was off the air!

"Oh, no!" I gasped, switching it off and running to the television set. "The monstrosity must have knocked out the transmitter." I'm sure my mouth formed itself into a soundless scream as my eyes widened in horror.

The deep baritone voice came in before the picture; "Now that Skylab is in its third orbit, we don't have long to wait."

"That's right, George," responded the other television reporter in a high tenor.

"And now, here's the west coast survival station." The picture flashed to an underground bomb shelter being renovated for survivors.

"What will happen next?" questioned the female reporter in a somber voice just outside the shelter. Then came a commercial.

Not trusting NASA, the television, or temporal existence, I decided to consult God. I knelt in front of the couch.

Folding my hands and closing my eyes tightly, I pleaded, "Save us! Oh, God, I know that the red on the doorposts saved the houses of Israel, the first Passover night in Egypt. And I realize that the scarlet cord hung out by Rahab saved herself and her family. Please, could you notice our red kitchen curtains and cause Skylab to pass us by?"

Feeling a shade better, I went into the kitchen to prepare dinner. Drawn to the radio switch as a moth is drawn to the flame, I turned it on.

I heard a discussion in progress: ". . . Skylab's trajectory could mean—"

"The doom of thousands of people," finished a nasal voice.

"O Lord," I whispered. "Forgive me for not thinking of the rest of the world. What will *they* do without crimson curtains?"

I glued my ear to the radio speaker as the reporters continued. We would have two hours' warning if we wanted to try to leave the area. I began to figure how far we'd get in two hours.

Next came a vivid description of the space station's enormous size—well, sort of enormous—along with a comparative view of Skylab or 1,000,000 tons of TNT exploding in my backyard.

Just then I heard the kids at the back door. "Hey, Mom! We're home!" Sounds of scuffling shoes and wet feet squishing up the stairs from swimming would have told me the same thing in a moment anyway.

"I'm home too," the soothing sound of my husband's voice called as he followed his sons up the stairs.

"Great!" I yelled excitedly. "You're just in time."

"Just in time for what?" inquired my darling spouse, wrapping both arms around me.

"You dare to get cuddly at a moment like this?" I looked at him in amazement. "Haven't you heard the news?"

"What news?" he asked, concerned.

"Skylab is in the third orbit." I lowered my voice to a whisper. I didn't want to panic the children.

"Are you still worrying about *Skylab*? It's a million to one chance," he concluded, opening the refrigerator door.

"Well, that's the one chance I'm concerned about," I replied evenly. "That's why I've made red kitchen curtains. Haven't you noticed?"

Taking him by the shoulders, I turned him toward the windows covered in fire-engine red. "What do you think?" I asked brightly.

"Are you kidding? What are these for?" He didn't seem to be pleased. "And what's the bumpy stuff on the bottom?" I held my breath as he walked slowly to the window and turned up the hemline. "And why the tape?" he queried.

"Never mind," I retorted. "I didn't have time to hem them properly—and you'll be sorry if Skylab hits and you have no protection."

He muttered something about me being enough protection for both of us and departed for his study.

Undaunted, I tried the boys next. "How do you like the new curtains, guys?"

"Yeah, nice, Mom," and they departed to ride their bikes. No one was interested in my curtains or Skylab. All they wondered about was supper. They got wieners.

About midnight, as I sat alone by the television keeping my vigil, a friend called on the telephone. At least *she* was worried. "Have you heard the latest report?"

"Yes, they're saying it'll hit Maine, but I'm praying it will land in the Indian Ocean."

She breathed a sigh of relief and said, "Good. I'm going to bed."

And I was left alone again. I wondered if Rahab had this much trouble with her family.

Just after two o'clock in the wee hours of the morning, the media signed off and left me with nothing but my fears and God.

I woke to hear birds chirping and felt sunshine streaming into the bedroom warming away the cool night air. Glancing at the clock, I saw it was after eight. Hearing the sounds of breakfast being prepared, I raced out to the kitchen.

"What happened?" I inquired of my husband.

"The kids are still sleeping," he replied.

"I don't mean the kids," I interjected. "I mean—"

"Skylab?" He finished the question for me. "It missed us."

"I know it missed us. We're still here, but where did it—"

"Land?" He casually dropped a piece of bread into the toaster. "It scattered itself all over a remote part of Australia."

"Thank goodness," I said, flopping into a chair.

"Red curtains wouldn't have made a difference," he laughingly commented.

"You just never mind," I shot back. "There's something about the color red, and I'm going to call the pastor today and find out what it is."

The pastor's voice carried a hint of laughter when he answered my query. "Red curtains wouldn't have made a difference because it wasn't the color that mattered, but the crimson blood of sacrifice needed to cover the sins of the people. You can read about it in Hebrews."[18]

Later I pondered as I put away the new curtains with the blouse in the bottom of the linen closet. What did it mean, "She fears not . . . for her household are *doubly* clothed in scarlet?" I knew that She knew. She had to have known.

But what about me?

FALL

9 / *Plowing*

"She considers a new field before she buys or accepts it."[19]

The bits of red and gold tipping the trees on the sides of the Chief reminded me that autumn had arrived. Feasting my eyes upon the changes in nature just outside my window, a wave of melancholy swept over me.

I stood with my arms crossed and complained, "I might as well try to move you, Chief, as to get people to listen to me. Now you," I hurried to explain, "at least *listen* to me even though you can't answer."

Reality gripped my heart.

"Yeah, I know," I went on, "and you're not going to answer this time, either, are you?"

John had hurriedly gulped his coffee that morning, anxious to get on to school and launch another year with new students and fresh challenges. In contrast, John Jr., Joe, and George had grumbled through their cold cereal and dragged their feet all the way to the car. And I had deposited each one.

Now I stood at the window and looked out upon the world. Silently I watched gaily colored leaves whirl in the wind, float past the window, and settle softly on the ground. "What a frail thing life is," I commented to my gigantic friend, "and how much there is to learn. Can I ever learn it in time?" My voice echoed the sadness sticking my heart, because deep down I felt that I could never change; I could never become like Her.

The telephone jarred me out of my reverie, and I rushed to answer it, glad for the interruption.

"Hello?" I cheerfully answered. Then I heard the voice of my dearest friend Jean saying, "Hello? Why didn't you say 'Hi'?"

"I'm glad you called. I was just thinking—"

"That's good for a Monday morning in September," she interjected.

"Never mind," I replied good-naturedly, "I want to ask you something. Did you know that eternity is like a fall sky?"

"What?" She was a close enough friend that she didn't bother to cover her bewilderment.

Without waiting for further encouragement, I began to explain. "I was just watching the autumn leaves, and I realized we are like those leaves because we are so feeble."

"I'm feeble this morning, I can tell you, after getting my kids off to school! When they—"

"You're not listening to me," I sighed.

Sensing I might really be upset, she decided to humor me. "What did you say?" she inquired more politely.

"I said we are feeble like fall leaves and that is a good thing. Leaves die and land in the grass and decay so that they can help the soil for the planting season that will come again in another year." I paused for a breath.

She yawned and responded, "I didn't know you were already getting into gardening for next spring. A little early, don't you think?"

"It has nothing to do with gardening," I curtly replied.

"Sorry," she said; then, "What *are* you talking about?"

"What I am trying to tell you is that eternity is like a fall sky. Don't you want to hear it?" My tone was menacing.

"Certainly." She sounded confused and concerned. "But do you feel all right?"

Happy to have her undivided attention at last, I plunged right ahead. "Eternity is like a fall sky because we think the trees are dying, but they are just pulling in their sap for the winter, and when the cold temperatures vanish, the trees come back to life."

"That's spring," she replied earnestly, trying to come in on the same wave length.

"That's right." Confidently I continued, "When we die, if we have believed in Jesus Christ and received His special kind of life, we are like those trees. We look dead on the outside, but our inside life will live on."

"I think I hear my doorbell. I'll have to go now." Instantly she hung up.

I felt crushed. I was obviously at odds with my environment. I wondered if there were really someone at her door.

Who could I call? Who would *listen* to me? I decided to try the pastor.

"Good morning!" the cheery voice boomed into the telephone.

"Why do people avoid serious subjects?" I inquired as soon as I had identified myself.

"What serious subjects are you trying to discuss?" he responded sympathetically.

"Eternity," I replied hopefully, assured this was a prime subject for him.

"Oh." He sounded tired all of a sudden.

"Listen," the pitch of my voice rose dangerously, "if I were trying to tell somebody I forgot my bread dough and it raised itself all over the oven rack, somebody would want to hear it. But if I want to tell somebody about eternity being like a fall sky, then the doorbell instantly has to be answered." Suddenly I wished I were an anonymous phone caller.

"Oh." The word sounded muffled.

"Would you like to know how eternity is like autumn?" I took a big breath and waited for his answer.

"Uh—oh. You'll never believe this, but I hear somebody pounding on the outer door of the church. It must be the secretary. I don't think I unlocked it," he concluded apologetically.

"Of course, I understand." But I didn't. The phone in my hand emitted a steady tone signalling the end of the conversation.

My isolation was complete. I went to the kitchen, made myself a cup of coffee, and picked up my Bible. Carefully turning the pages to avoid Proverbs 31, I came across, "No one, after putting his hand to the plow and looking back, is fit for the kingdom of God."[20]

The verse leaped off the page at me. "That's it!" I exclaimed triumphantly. Awed by my discovery, I leaned back in my chair and sipped my coffee reflectively. I'd been feeling like I was plowing a field harder than the earth I'd dug up for my strawberry patch. At the same time I had felt as though my feet were sticking in mud which threatened to suck my shoes off with each step. I'd never felt more alone. Then I realized, as I set my coffee cup down on the kitchen counter, that a farmer didn't feel at odds with his fields; he just plowed them. I chewed it over in my brain. "Each of us has a different field to plow. I can't expect other people to fully understand where I am, what I am doing, and thinking, and saying." I was speaking to myself slowly, softly, thrilled by my discovery. Then I closed my Bible and hugged it close.

Much relieved, I walked over to the picture window which framed the Chief. For some reason unknown to me, I no longer felt alone. I spied a white gull soaring above the river which flowed along the base of the Chief. My eyes followed the bird's path until it became a speck in the sky, then vanished.

The Chief faded from view as my mind's eye instead pictured a prairie at day's end, the fading sun streaking the sky with lovely hues of pink, powder blue and lavender over an empty cornfield. The rich, dark soil stretched out before me almost to infinity. Standing there, on the edge of the field, I could see many plowed furrows on either side of me. Thousands of rows seemed to fill the huge field. The area before me, however, was untouched by plow or hoe.

Where the heavens met the horizon, I could barely make out the end of my section. "It's so long," I said with discouragement.

In my vision I turned my head to the left and then to the right and saw no one—only plowed ridges as far as my eyes could see.

Then I realized that an infinite number of Christians must have previously plowed the ditches on either side of my unworked area. The only untouched surface was mine. Before me stood an unused plow.

The hand cultivator beckoned me to grab hold and begin. I considered the field. Did I have a choice? To say no to a call for hard work and service was to deny my Lord. He called me to refuse a life of ease and go forward. I could not wait. My identity lay in Jesus who gave me life and waited at the other end. The harvest would be for Him. I stepped forward and reached out to grasp the handle.

My daydream evaporated at the clang of the telephone. "Mom"—I heard the anxious voice of George—"did you forget I have to go to the dentist to get my braces checked?"

"Oh, no!" I replied in shock. "I'll be right there!"

Sprinting down the stairs, I grabbed the keys on my way past the table, wrestled the door open, and scrambled into the car. Roaring down the street, I felt great about life even though I felt terrible about forgetting my son's dental appointment. I screeched to a halt in front of the elementary school and opened the door for George.

"Sorry, dear!" I quickly apologized, as he climbed into the car.

"That's okay," he replied cheerfully, strapping on his seat belt without being reminded.

"Would you like to hear about eternity, and an autumn sky?" I couldn't wait to share my morning's discoveries.

He simply looked at me. From past experience he knew I would tell him anyway.

"Motherhood can be wonderful," I started over as the vision of the beckoning plow flashed into my mind.

"Are you okay?" he inquired with sincere interest. "I thought you were going to tell me about some kind of sky, and then you started talking about motherhood."

"Sorry, sweetie." I patted his arm. "I was just thinking out loud."

He nodded agreeably, trying to pick a safe course in some uncharted waters.

"Anyway," I went on, "it's not important. I'd just rather tell you what a good boy you are and how much I love you."

"Thanks, Mom!" his shiny metal grin spanned the width of his face.

"Here's the dentist's office," I announced to George's considerable relief.

Walking into the office, my nose was assaulted by the smell of alcohol and leather furniture. Seated in one of the lined-up chairs was my friend Jean. "Well, hello! Fancy meeting you here" was my original line. I could see her eyeing me suspiciously and recalled she had hung up on me earlier.

"I had a dental appointment," she offered defensively.

I understood her anxiety. She was afraid I was going to let loose with some more of my "eternity-like-a-fall-sky" philosophy. "George had to have his wiring checked out. Maybe his overbite is now an underbite," I joked to alert her to the fact that I'd changed since our earlier conversation. I picked up a magazine and flipped through the pages.

"I didn't mean to cut you off on the telephone," she began apologetically.

"It's all right, I understand." I reached over and patted her on the arm.

"Would you like to tell me about the autumn sky now?" she asked in a I'll-do-it-if-I-have-to tone.

Thinking of my vision of the plow and recalling that part of service is consideration of the feelings of others, I giggled inwardly to myself and said, "I've changed my thinking about that."

"George?" The voice of the dental assistant interrupted our talk.

Smiling at my youngest son, I watched him disappear behind the door. I felt proud of his bravery in the presence of all those gleaming instruments of torture.

"Listen"—she leaned closer and lowered her voice—"I've been thinking about what you were saying. I guess sometimes I feel too busy to think about eternity."

"I've learned something from you too," I responded. "You know, service with a smile works in the Christian life as well as in businesses. You're always ready to listen to me, and I'm thankful for that. You're a good friend; one I treasure."

Her eyes opened wide in surprise. She wasn't used to me

showing much affection. "Thank you," she replied. "I've always thought you were pretty special too."

"Mrs. Marks?" The dental assistant again cut into our conversation.

"See you later," she whispered quickly, and then disappeared behind the beige door which had swallowed George.

My heart was light as I returned home with my youngest one's mouth tightened anew by stronger wires. I hurried to prepare dinner. I knew my husband wanted to eat on time for a change; he had papers to grade.

Later the boys were in bed and I sat knitting as John came into the living room to join me. "All through studying for tonight?" I inquired.

"As through as I intend to be," he replied. He kissed me on the top of my head and stretched out on the sofa.

"Did you ever read Proverbs 31:16?" I tried to sound offhand and didn't look up from my knitting.

"I suppose so," he answered; "why?" He closed his eyes and yawned.

I gave a reply which surprised even me. "Just wondering. You're tired. Why don't you close your eyes for a while?" Teaching all day and studying at night drained him both mentally and physically. Normally I would have resented his yawn at my question. The plow, however, reminded me of service.

Gratefully he blew me a kiss and soon was off in dreamland.

I finished the pattern I was knitting and then tiptoed out to the kitchen to read my Bible before I turned out the lights. Opening the book to Proverbs, I read, "She considers a new field before she buys or accepts it—expanding prudently [and not courting neglect of her pressent duties by assuming others]. With her savings [of time and strength] she plants fruitful vines in her vineyard."[21]

I paused for a moment and thought about Her. Not wanting to precipitate a dream attack, however, I looked up a reference listed along with the verse, Song of Solomon 8:12 in the Amplified: "You, O Solomon, can have your thousand, and those who tend the fruit of it two hundred; but my vineyard, which is mine [with all its radiant joy], is before me!"

Peace flooded over me as I realized the truth of what I'd read. That morning the vision of the plow had established my thoughts. I knew that to really serve Jesus Christ, I would have to learn to plow deep rather than wide. And in reading the Bible just now, it dawned upon me that my row began at home.

My vineyard surrounded me! Excitement lifted me up as I turned out the lights in the kitchen and hurried into the living room to wake my sleeping spouse.

I was surprised to find him already sound asleep—in bed. I wondered how he'd managed to get from the living room to our bedroom without my hearing him. "I was probably concentrating too hard on my thoughts," I muttered as I turned out the light and crawled into bed for the night.

"Did you read your verse, honey?" he mumbled before he began to snore.

"I got it now," I replied enthusiastically. "You just pick up the plow and go for it."

His breathing slowed down, then deepened, and he slumbered in peace.

It didn't matter, because I didn't feel alone anymore. As I pulled the covers up around his shoulders, I murmured, "It's just you and me, Lord. You, me, and the plow."

10 / Battle

"She will comfort, encourage and do him only good as long as there is life within her."[22]

"Jelly in the jar," I sang enthusiastically while I stirred the grape juice beginning to bubble in the pot. "Jelly in the jar—oh, what fun! Har-dee-har-har . . ." I smiled contentedly at my inventiveness both in making jam at 6:30 a.m. and in creating a song at the same time.

John appeared in the kitchen doorway.

"Did your nose wake you up?" I smiled my welcome.

"Smells good," he answered. "What is it?" My husband walked over next to me and wrapped an arm around my waist.

After giving him a quick kiss, I returned to my cooking. "I'm making grape jelly for your toast this morning, and I love you very much," I said happily. It was a special moment by the stove.

"Thanks!" he grinned. "On both counts."

"Uh, oh, I have to time the boiling." I reached in my house-coat pocket for Joe's stopwatch. Normally it was used for his sporting events at school. Timing and stirring at the same time, completely engrossed in jelly making, I exclaimed over its beauty as I clicked the watch off after exactly one minute.

"See, honey? My first batch of grape jelly." I proudly announced the completion of the process. Hearing no response, I turned around to discover that I was again alone. I didn't want to wake the kids by calling for him to come and see the luscious concoction, so I decided to look for him.

Where can he be? I thought to myself as I searched. *This house isn't that large.* Then I heard the shower turn on in the bathroom. "I know what I'll do," I whispered to myself. "I'll go and get the morning paper for him so he'll have it as soon as he comes out of the shower. I'm sure he will like that." I skipped down the basement stairs humming my "Jelly in the jar . . ."

On the way to the back door, I spotted a pool of water on the laundry room floor near the washing machine. My mind immediately connected the water running upstairs in the bathroom with the puddle on the floor. I went to investigate. "Humm," I deduced, "there's the liquid; now, where's the leak?"

Looking up at the ceiling, I spied water dripping from a copper pipe. "Oh, no!" I exclaimed. "The shower is leaking!" I didn't know what to do next—whether to warn John immediately of impending disaster—a flood on the floor—or to get him the newspaper.

I decided to do both.

Hurrying to the back door, I whipped it open, grabbed the paper from the carport floor where our new paperboy liked to fling it, and ran into the house, slamming the door behind me. I heard the door bounce, but not shut. "Oh, well," I muttered, "I'll come back and close it as soon as I tell John about the leaky pipe."

Racing up the stairs two at a time, I stubbed my toe on the second step from the top, and hobbled to the bathroom.

Opening the door, I let in a rush of cold air. "John," I called into a cloud of steam, "turn off the shower. It's leaking water all over the floor downstairs."

"The water's what?" He hollered over the pelting spray.

"It's leaking all over the floor!" I yelled back.

"What's happening?" John Jr. shouted from the hall.

I spoke sharply to the intruding voice. "It's nothing. Go back to bed."

"But it's time to get *up!*" he retorted.

"Well, then, get up!" I snarled, glaring at him. "But do it in your room. We already have enough trouble!" My concluding remarks ended in a high-pitched shriek. Turning my attention back to John, I bellowed, "John, you've got to do something about him! He doesn't listen . . ."

"Would you please lower your voice?" John's quiet voice interrupted my ear-piercing tirade. Suddenly I realized the water was off.

Calming myself, I took a deep breath and in controlled tones explained, "John, I came in here to tell you that water is pouring down from the shower onto the floor downstairs—near the washing machine." He poked his head out from behind the shower curtain in alarm.

"How much water?" he asked in concern.

"Enough," I stated, my hands on my hips, "to warrant my informing you. But maybe you're not interested in that. *Or in the fact that your son yells at me whenever I speak to him.*" I crossed my arms in front of me and stood firmly on both feet for the final summation. "I left my jam to—" I froze for a moment as my mind flashed before me a picture of grape goop—possibly black, charred, gummy goop—all over the stove and the floor. Dropping the newspaper, I bolted out of the bathroom.

No, no, no! my mind screamed as I ran at breakneck speed for the jelly I'd left. Rushing into the kitchen, I ran straight to the stove and the disaster.

What's this? I puzzled in amazement. I stared at the gleaming pan filled to the brim with purple jelly. *What? I hadn't ruined the jam!* Somehow I'd managed to think of turning off the burner before I went downstairs. I swayed a little. *I need to sit down,* I reasoned, heading for the living room.

Passing Joe's hamster cage, I noticed "Hampst the Great" sleeping soundly. His nose tucked into his soft fur, he looked completely comfortable. "That's what I should be doing," I said to the snoozing ball of fluff.

I flopped down on the sofa and threw my feet up on the coffee table. I felt exhausted. "Whew! That was a close call," I said breathing a sigh of relief.

"I thought you were making jam," quipped John as he hurried past the living room to the laundry room. Less than a minute later he stood before me. "There is nothing wrong down there," he announced with irritation in his voice. "Nothing I can fix, that is."

"Then what was the water I saw? There was some dripping off a copper pipe just above a *huge* puddle on the floor. Surely you can fix the pipe, can't you?"

"How about training the dog," he replied in a sarcastic tone. "The puddle is his. The drip you saw was only a little condensation." He shot a look of disgust in my direction.

Remembering our recent dispute about Johnny's dog, Specimen, using the floor as her relief station, I bristled. John felt the dog should always stay outside because of her gigantic size. I felt that Specimen should be taught to control herself while inside the house. "It couldn't have been Specimen!" I snapped. "She's been outside since yesterday."

Speaking to me as if I were a student failing a course, he replied, "You left the door open when you went outside to get this morning's paper."

His tone of accusation pushed me over the edge. I bared my teeth and growled, "I wasn't getting the morning paper for *me*. I was getting it for *you*!" I leaned back on the couch in satisfaction. *Let him top that one!* I thought.

"Martha," he responded, lowering his voice, "if you were ever *up* in the morning before I had to leave for work, you would know that I don't have time to read the paper before I leave. I'm too busy feeding the boys." With that blow, he turned on his heel and left the room.

I jumped off the couch as if hit by a bolt of electricity. My mind reeled in pain. *How unfair! How could he say such a mean thing?* I knew that morning wasn't my prime time, but I'd been trying to get up lately. I could feel angry tears threatening to fill my eyes. *How could he have humiliated me that way?*

With as much dignity as I could muster, I walked deliberately to the kitchen to pour the cooled jelly into the jars.

Thankful to have something to do with my hands, I managed to pour the melted paraffin onto the hot jelly, sealing the jars.

Then I furiously beat eggs in a bowl, poured them into a skillet, and waited for them to scramble.

I popped the bread into the toaster and fumed.

Speaking to no one, I slammed the dishes and silverware on the table and poured the orange juice and milk.

"Breakfast is ready!" I yelled.

John appeared at the table first, looking quite cool and collected. I marveled at how I could love him one minute and want to strangle him the next. He had the slightly damp newspaper with him. He opened it up in front of his face and stared at the soggy print.

Sitting down at the other end of the table, I imagined how good it would feel to toss a few scrambled eggs right into the center of the paper, but immediately rejected violence as an alternative. I settled for a slow burn—with revenge to be served later.

The boys straggled to the table in various stages of dress. When they were all seated, I ordered, "George, you say grace."

"Me?" he whined. "But Daddy always—"

"Your mother said *you*," interjected John firmly.

Puzzled, George mumbled something about being grateful.

I immediately felt a stab of pain. *Why is it adults have to hurt their children by acting like children?* I wondered. I wanted to close the gap with John, but his stinging remark still hurt too much. I said nothing.

John Jr., seemingly unaware of our feud, inhaled his eggs with the determination of a boa constrictor swallowing its prey, and downed his juice in one gulp.

Joe wouldn't eat anything. He had a track meet first thing in the morning. "It slows down my running, Mom. By the way— are you through with my stopwatch?"

Handing him the timepiece, I refused to quarrel with him over food. Tangling with John had been more than enough for one morning.

George also refused to eat—"mushy eggs that slip around on a plate." I let that pass too.

John said nothing more than "please pass the salt."

I felt too wounded to want any breakfast. I watched as John helped himself to my freshly made grape jelly, and I sulked silently. Mounded on top of his toast, it sparkled, jiggled and mocked my efforts to be a good wife like Her. I relished my wrath and decided to bide my time for revenge until later in the day.

Breakfast over, John announced, "I'll take the boys to school this morning."

"Fine," I said in clipped tones. *He probably didn't think I could handle the job,* I thought. I began to clear away the breakfast dishes and busy myself with trips back and forth to the kitchen.

As soon as they were gone, I laid my head down and cried. Tears of anger and frustration poured out. *"I will never be like Her,"* I sobbed. I felt as though I were being ripped in two. Half of me wanted to get even with John, but the other half seemed to say, "Never mind. Just love him."

"I do love him. It's just that I can't stand him today." There was no humor in my response. I identified with the Apostle Paul when he said, "Wretched man that I am! Who will set me free from the body of this death?"[23]

I'd learned at Bible study that at one time when a murderer was convicted of killing a person, the punishment often used was to strap the dead body onto the killer's back. When the corpse decayed, the murderer slowly sickened and died.

I knew that my old life was like that, and I desperately wanted to be free from my temper and unkindness to my family. I'd decided to put my hand to the plow, but this first hard spot I'd hit in my unplowed heart of selfishness and self-centeredness was awful. I wanted to return to my old ways of handling things. *She* was tearing me in two.

Before Her, I would have enjoyed a couple days of pouting, and then would have caused John to pay dearly for hurting my feelings. (I had my ways.) But then She came along. Now I didn't want to get even, but I didn't want to hurt either!

That liberated woman of Proverbs 31 had gotten me into something I couldn't handle. "I was better off knowing nothing than knowing something that I can't do," I complained to myself.

I needed someone, or something, to blame.

The Chief would do nicely. "Well, Chief," I addressed the monolith from the safety of my living room, "it may have been She who got me into this, but it's all *your* fault." The words tumbled out all at once.

The Chief said nothing.

"How can anybody have a decent outlook on life living next to you? No view, zero visability, fog, rain, hail, and floods," I stormed. "No wonder people want to leave this disgusting area. It's unfit for human habitation!"

Fog drifted slowly in front of the mountain and began to obscure my view of the usually beloved scene. Eventually realizing the futility of spouting off at an inanimate object, I charged angrily out to the kitchen.

The sparkling jelly glasses neatly lined up on the kitchen counter caused the war within me to escalate. Rage rioted against love. Love, always the stronger, was about to win.

"I must think this through calmly," I said to myself. "What is all the fuss about?" My voice sounded almost like I imagined Hers would sound.

He insulted you! Remember that? my mind shouted.

I grabbed the bottle of Jubilant dishwashing liquid, the happy soap which needed no help to clean the dirtiest of grime, and I prayed. "Help me, Lord. I can't stand myself."

The quiet voice inside said, "You can choose to wallow in your pain and hurt, or you can choose to forgive and love. Which will it be?" Tears of release welled up in my eyes as I surrendered to love.

My prayer was answered. Love replaced revenge. My balance was restored to serenity. "Thank you, God," I whispered.

God had heard my cry, and He cared. Peace wrapped its arms around me and lifted my spirit high above myself into God's love.

While I stood at the kitchen sink scraping eggs off the skillet and scouring the pan to a high shine, I thought about my argument with John. What had happened between our warmth over the jelly pan and his jab about fixing breakfast? Could I honor him as the head of our home as I honored Jesus Christ as Lord of my life? Could I willingly submit to his authority all the time?

For every question I asked myself, I came up with two different answers—mine and Hers.

I realized that She would always see the best in Her mate.

Getting even for a real or imagined insult probably wouldn't even cross Her mind.

But what about me? I knew I wanted to be like Her, and that desire grew stronger each day. Often I could see Her in my mind and sense Her drawing me out of my old ways. I could feel Her standing next to me, suggesting kindness instead of cruelty.

"You've got to want something enough to pay the price to attain it. That's the first step toward the goal," I comforted and encouraged myself. She must have had to begin somewhere, and her husband probably wasn't perfect either.

After I'd wiped the dishes and was stacking them neatly in the cupboard, it hit me. My heart leaped with the discovery. *The puddle was already on the floor when I went to get the newspaper for John!*

I couldn't believe it, but it was true. Specimen *couldn't* have made the puddle. My leaving the door open had nothing to do with it.

"John was wrong," I said slowly. "Utterly and completely wrong!"

Temptation whispered, "Now's your chance. Nail him when he walks through the door tonight."

NO! I thought. I will try, especially in the light of this revelation, to act like Her.

I prepared John his favorite dessert, apple pie, and after he and the boys had finished dinner, I helped the kids do their homework so he could work on his thesis. John seemed quiet. *Probably waiting for me to get even,* I figured.

As soon as the boys were in bed, I went to John's study to talk to him. He appeared extremely busy and ignored my presence. I could have left him to his misery, but I knew that She would probably humble herself so he could save face.

After standing for a long moment, I broke the silence. "How's the research coming?" I tried to sound casual.

"Okay," he answered without looking up from his book.

"I'm sorry about this morning," I said. It was the most difficult pronouncement of my life. He had falsely accused me, and I was apologizing to *him*! Suddenly a great flood of love filled my heart. I waited for him to respond.

"I'm sorry too," he replied gently. And in less than two shakes of a lamb's tail, we were hugging each other like high school sweethearts.

Knowing how much I loved buttery popcorn, John said, "Let's go make your favorite snack—with *lots* of butter!"

"Great idea," I agreed.

While we were working side by side in the kitchen, I felt something was bothering John. "Anything on your mind?" I inquired, melting some butter in a small saucepan.

He looked sheepishly at me. "I've got a confession to make."

"What?" I said.

"Specimen didn't make that puddle on the floor. George did."

"George?" I almost dropped the spoon.

"Yes. He told me about it on the way to school this morning. It seems he spilled his bubble-maker last night on the floor near the washing machine. He was afraid to tell us this morning, he said, because 'you were both so mad.' "

"You mean we had all that fuss over a puddle of *soapy water*?" I smoothed my eyebrows with my index finger, and rubbed my nose with my wrist in amazement.

"Guess so," he responded with a rueful grin.

"You know what, John?" I put the spoon down on the kitchen counter and stood next to him.

"What?" he inquired with a twinkle in his eye.

"You make the best popcorn in the whole world!" I threw both arms around his neck and hugged him tightly.

"And you make the best jam," he replied, giving me a bear hug.

"Jelly," I corrected.

"Jelly," he agreed.

Somewhere in the eternal spheres, She smiled.

11 / Abide

"She looks for wool and flax, and works with her hands in delight. She is like merchant ships; she brings her food from afar."[24]

I woke up shivering. *What had I done wrong?* I wondered. Reaching for the alarm clock, I squinted at its face in the early morning light. *Five-thirty!* I thought in amazement.

Then it hit me. I'd had another dream about Her.

But I've been doing so well. Confused, I tried to collect my thoughts. Mentally I accused the empty popcorn bowl of drugging me into a dream attack. *It must be the popcorn,* I reasoned, putting the alarm clock back on the night table.

I tried to recall the will-o'-the-wisp phantom which had destroyed my spiritual peace. Nothing.

"I hate it when John is away for mayor meetings," I muttered to myself. The house felt cold, and I shivered. Snuggling under my comforter until only my nose showed, I stared wide-eyed at the ceiling, trying to remember the dream.

Zero recall. Only vague feelings of discomfort akin to guilt. Unable to sleep, I sat up and turned on the light. I picked up my Bible and opened quickly to Proverbs 31—and Her. The words jumped off the page and hit me right where it hurt: "Give her of the fruit of her hands; and let her own works praise her in the gates."[25]

Closing the book, I threw the comforter over my head as last night's dream flashed before my eyes. She had been canning the fruits of God's Holy Spirit. I watched as She stood on a fluffy cloud surrounded by cherubs. One by one, she deposited *peace, joy, patience, love, self-control, kindness, faithfulness, goodness,* and *gentleness* into translucent containers. A chime played softly each time the product touched the bottom.

Beads of perspiration popped out along my hairline. It took me a moment to realize that the comforter over my nose was overheating and almost smothering me.

"That's it. I've had it!" I grumbled to myself as I rolled over and out of bed.

Stomping out to the kitchen, flipping up the thermostat for heat along the way, I filled the teakettle and turned the burner on high.

"I'll fix *Her*," I vowed. "I can come up with a few fruits of my own!"

The die was cast.

When the boys appeared for breakfast, they couldn't believe their eyes. There stood their mother wearing a brilliant blue satin dress with a pink rose the size of a grapefruit on the left hip. I was teetering dangerously on heels four inches high.

"You gonna wear that all day, Mom?" inquired George carefully.

"What's that funny blue stuff around your eyes, Mom?" questioned Joe.

"I think she looks nice," defended John Jr. in worried tones. He glared at his brothers.

"Thank you," I replied sweetly.

Now that that was over, George tried to steer things in a more normal direction. "Pow-Wow again! I hate Pow-Wow," he complained.

"Uh, oh," said Joe.

"Pow-Wow? Thanks, Mom," interjected John Jr. bravely. "This is better than the hot dogs and peanut butter we had yesterday. How'd you do it?"

"If you're not in the mood for Pow-Wow, George, my love, I could prepare for your culinary enjoyment an egg, perhaps two," I answered with confidence.

George's eyes grew bigger than his glasses. Bewildered, he

glanced at John Jr. for support and responded, "Uh, Pow-Wow is fine, Mom."

"Then let's eat," I chirped blithely.

"What's for lunch?" asked George, spooning half the sugar bowl onto his bowl of steaming cereal.

"Baloney on rye with mustard," I stated musically.

"Oh," they replied sadly.

"George"—I leaned my elbows on the table and folded my hands under my chin—"I have a surprise for you. I'm going to clean Ben's cage today."

The spoon stopped in midair. "You're gonna clean my guinea pig's cage?" His mouth dropped open. He glanced at Joe who refused to look up from his bowl. "Uh, thanks, Mom!" His glasses slid down his nose, and he attacked his breakfast with passion.

"Joe." I addressed him pointedly. He refused to raise his eyes to meet my steady gaze. "I'll deliver your newspapers for you after school. I know you've been working hard on your school-work lately." I overlooked the tablespoon of jam he plopped onto his Pow-Wow and turned my attention to John Jr.

"For you, my sweet angel, I also have a small contribution. You recall that term paper you've been struggling to type?"

"Yes," he answered slowly, pausing in mid-bite.

"Consider it done." Beaming, I leaned back in my chair.

"Are you gonna be mayor for Daddy too?" innocent George inquired.

They each glanced at me quickly, waiting for the explosion.

"Daddy is already doing that—out of town," I replied, still syrupy sweet.

"Well," I said, "if there's nothing else, and you have all finished eating, I'll drive you to school now." I pushed my chair back, stood up, and stumbled slightly when my heel caught in the rug.

All three boys rushed to my aid, but I waved them off with a grand gesture. I straightened my dress and responded with, "Just leave the dishes. I'll get them later."

I walked slowly down the steps, trying not to cling too tightly to the handrail. I held out my coat to John Jr. and thanked him graciously as he tried to balance his schoolbooks and help me at the same time.

As the boys tumbled out of the house and into the car, I carefully balanced an imaginary pile of books on top of my head (like a model learning to walk) and glided. I gracefully stepped into the automobile full of rather subdued boys.

Instead of becoming upset and angry when my seat belt remained stuck in the car door after I'd shut it, I kept quiet and casually reopened the door to retrieve the errant belt. I reminded myself that patience was a virtue.

The drive to school was uneventful.

"Bye! Have a blessed day!" I warbled at each stop. Then I aimed the car for home.

Arriving back a little later than usual because I'd kept to the speed limit, I really had to scurry in order to clean up the kitchen before 10 a.m., my customary deadline.

The telephone rang just as I was tottering to put away the toaster.

"Good morning," I sang, "whoever you are—"

"I'm sorry. I have the wrong number." The voice of my dearest friend, Jean Marks, sounded confused.

"No, you don't, my sweet! And how are you this fine morning?" My voice was music to my ears.

"I know," she said eagerly, suddenly enthusiastic; "you've won the grocery store draw!"

"No, I haven't. Guess again," I replied mysteriously.

"Someone delivered a million dollars to your door?" Her curiosity was tickling me.

"Nope," I answered, "but almost." I sang the words. "Do you recall inviting me to join the women's movement in town to fight against almost everything and reform the rest?"

"Yes," she responded. "And *you* said women should stay home and bake bread and improve their outlook on life."

"Well, rejoice, my dear, because I've changed my mind. I'm going to help your cause. I have a few things to do here at home, but as soon as I get organized, I'll be right over. See you in an hour." I ignored the stunned silence at the other end of the telephone receiver and hurriedly hung up. I could hardly wait to shock them all with my overflowing virtue.

Humming away, I teetered back and forth from the table to the kitchen, clearing away the breakfast dishes. Stacking them in the sink, I hobbled as quickly as possible to the bathroom to check my face and hairdo. "Not bad," I humbly announced to my reflection.

The guinea pig! As fast as four-inch heels would allow, I wobbled to the kitchen to get him a carrot.

"Listen, Ben," I crooned in a soothing tone, "you'll have to wait for a while, but later I will create a clean home for you."

Ben squealed.

Oh, no, the term paper! Remembering I'd promised to type John Jr.'s term paper, I figured I'd better at least find it before I left for the women's meeting at Jean's house. *Where does he keep his term paper?* I fought down the rising frustration as I plowed through his desk drawers. "Eraser, scissors, calculator, a rusty quarter, two teeth, and a piece of siding from somebody's house," I mumbled, digging through a mass of crumpled papers. "Where would he put his term paper?" I asked myself. I glanced at his clock ticking away on his bedside table. "Eleven-thirty!" I said in shock. *Better do it later,* I decided.

Meanwhile, my friend Jean was so thrilled to think that at last I would cooperate with the women working to free other women and men and children, dogs, and cats, that she had gathered a few ladies for coffee at her house.

"We call it a *driving committee*," she patiently explained as soon as I'd stepped into her living room. I decided to forget the fact that the guinea pig cage was uncleaned and that I failed to find the term paper before I left home.

I'm not certain how it happened, but before I knew what had happened I'd volunteered to lead the pack of ladies in their quest to close down the highway leading out of town, which my husband, the mayor, was fighting to keep open for reasons I never had clearly understood.

The principle behind the driving committee's aim to close down the highway resulted from a recent washout in which two people had died. They wanted to force people in power to build another road. When I thought about it later, I realized that John believed keeping the highway open was important because it was the only road leading out of town. However, I wasn't thinking . . .

It made sense to me that I would lead the demonstration. We would stand in the middle of the highway so that the cars trying to use the road would either hit us or stop.

"And you'll be there at 4:00 p.m. sharp. That's prime drive-time." Jean's voice filtered into my foggy brain. "Agreed?"

"Agreed!" I vehemently exclaimed.

"Glad to have you with us." She gazed warmly around the room at the other women sipping coffee and nodding appreciatively in my direction.

Their approval warmed my soul. "Thank you," I replied purely. I was enjoying the bond brought about by a common foe—the highway. John's leadership in our town or in our home simply was not a consideration.

The rest of the day went as scheduled. I cleaned Ben's cage, picked up the boys after school, and even delivered newspapers for Joe. I asked John Jr. where his term paper was. I should have known—under his bed. I managed to prepare supper for the boys before it was time to set up the roadblock.

"Just put your term paper in Daddy's study," I trilled to John Jr. "Be sure to eat a good supper. I'll see you after we close down the road. It shouldn't take long," I stated confidently as I tripped quickly down the stairs barely touching the handrail.

Somewhat bewildered but rather accustomed to it by now, the boys chorused, "Okay, Mom."

Pride lifted my self-image as I drove to the main intersection of town. The other girls were already there with placards and flags, walking slowly back and forth in the crosswalk without waiting for the walk light.

Parking the car by the side of the road, I tottered over in my heels to my place at the head of the line. Jean pressed a banner in my hands, saying, "Hold this high so that everyone can see it. We're getting television coverage too."

Standing in the middle of the road in my brilliant blue satin dress with a now slightly crushed pink rose, I felt that my past was behind me. I was holy like Her.

We managed to close the road for two hours, and I was personally interviewed by a television news reporter. Our small riot was successful. Traffic was snarled for twenty miles on either side of town. Somehow, though, something didn't seem quite right . . .

Long after the boys were in bed and asleep, I sat pecking away at John's typewriter, typing John Jr.'s report. I collapsed into bed and was asleep almost before my head hit the pillow.

Next morning the boys were excited. "Dad will be home today!" John Jr. yelled.

The pain in my feet detered any attempt at conversation on my part as I struggled to get through the morning routine. Dark circles ringed my eyes, replacing the cosmetic shadow. My back felt as though it had developed a permanent sway.

Somehow I didn't look forward to seeing John.

As soon as I'd delivered the boys to school, I hurried to my Bible. There it was in Proverbs 31:13, 14: She found wool and flax and turned it into a product while she felt "delight."

I felt miserable, but I wasn't sure why.

And then, it said, She was like a merchant ship bringing food from afar.

"I stopped food from coming into town." I painfully recalled the picture of the huge van being turned away, full of goods for the supermarket. Shame flushed my cheeks.

Fatigue, and the sudden realization of my true behavior forced the floodwaters to break.

"God," I sobbed, "what happened?" Suddenly the vision of me parading around sickened my soul.

"I did everything, Lord!" I sat like a penitent child with my hands folded in my lap. "I loved you, God. I followed you the best I could—I was peaceful under stress, joyful under discomfort, patient when I wanted to scream. Wasn't that like Her fruit?"

"You can't *produce* fruit; you must *bear* it," a voice deep inside my soul seemed to say.

Silently I thumbed through the pages before me to Psalm 91. "He who dwells in the shelter of the Most High will abide in the shadow of the Almighty."[26]

"How will I get to the shelter, Lord?" I whispered, turning more pages.

"He who has found his life shall lose it, and he who has lost his life for My sake shall find it."[27]

I was alone in the house, but I began to sense another presence in the bedroom with me. A quietness, a peace began to wrap itself around me as I reflected upon the One who had created me and given me life. My Bible became the living Word to me as I read in John 15:5, "He who abides in Me, and I in him, he bears much fruit; for apart from Me you can do nothing."[28]

No more fighting. I felt refreshed as I realized that I could not bear fruit unless I would abide in Jesus Christ. *Abiding is not a production, but a condition,* came the dawning realization, *almost like a state of being.*

How had this all started? I tried to remember my flippant declaration: "I'll fix Her—I can come up with a few fruits of my own!"

Remorse over my actions swept away the last wisps of pride as I sadly saw myself as God must have seen me. I was busy "for Him" (I had said) while being totally preoccupied with myself. I was so full of me and my own activities that I hadn't had time to wonder what God thought about what I was doing.

"What am I going to tell John when he comes home today?"

"That's what I've accomplished, Lord—nothing." Tears rolled gently down my cheeks.

"But, Lord," I sniffed and blew my nose, "how did *She* do it?"

Silence.

Sensing that I might be off on the wrong track again, I flipped around in my Bible concordance for the word "abide." "The one who says he abides in Him ought himself to walk in the same manner as He walked."[29]

What were some things Jesus had done? I remembered that He had washed the feet of His disciples out of love.

Aha! I was on my way to the basement for dark shoe polish. My spirits lifted a little as I found the shoes John had been meaning to shine. While I rubbed the polish into the shoe leather, I thought about the word "abide." I figured it meant to continue in a stable state, but what else?

My old stand-by, the dog-eared dictionary, had a few more answers. To abide meant to wait expectantly; to face or submit to without shrinking; to bear patiently; to stand the consequences of; or to suffer for something.

As I shined my husband's shoes with a brush and then with a soft cloth, I realized that *abide* was something I had to do, not something I could feel.

Abiding meant that I had to step out of myself and into Jesus Christ. I was to be the branch, not the vine. Yes, I loved Him, even had tried to serve Him; but *He* was the Source of life, not me.

I also realized I had to apologize to John. I had acted against his better interests. It was a bitter pill, but one I knew I had to swallow if I were ever to be like Her.

John arrived home after the kids were already asleep. I served him a piece of homemade apple pie, his favorite, as sort of a peace offering. We sat across the table from each other in silence.

"I saw you on television today," he said quietly, his eyes dark with hurt.

"I know," I answered with my head down. Tears suddenly filled my eyes, and I confessed all that I had done in his absence.

John listened attentively all the way through, and then he forgave me. But inside I still hurt.

Later that night when not a creature in our house stirred, I lay awake thinking. *Abiding in God's love will be the test of my character. Character, not emotion, will demonstrate whether or not I am walking as Jesus walked.*

I realized I couldn't walk His way under my own power because His way led to the cross. I could never go there under my own steam.

"Lord," I whispered into the darkness of our bedroom, "I don't know much about the way of the cross. But I know that you know and that She must have known. Prepare me, Lord Jesus. I want to bear fruit for you."

My prayer was about to be answered.

WINTER

12 / Pruning

"She tastes and sees that her gain from work [with and for God] is good; her lamp goes not out; but it burns on continually through the night [of trouble, privation or sorrow, warning away fear, doubt and distrust]."[30]

"Quick, Mom! Get up. There's snow on the Chief!" Into my bedroom leaped George—superhero style. He touched down with a loud thump about a foot from my head.

"George, what-is-your-problem?" I moaned.

His delighted expression faded. "I just wanted you to know that there's snow on the Chief," he replied defensively.

"Couldn't you tell me *later* on a Saturday morning?" I pulled myself up to a sitting position. My head ached strangely.

"Anyway," he smiled with all the charm he could muster, "Daddy said I could wake you up. He just left for the mountains a couple minutes ago." Superhero stood on one foot and then the other, fending off imaginary enemies.

I remembered. John had been hoping for good snow cover all week. Getting away into the white world of clean air and powdery trails refreshed him for the tough days of winter when absenteeism was ravaging the high school because of colds and flu. I would have the boys all by myself. Ignoring my pounding head, I crawled out of bed and asked, "Snow on the Chief? Why didn't you tell me?"

His face lit up when he saw that I was interested. He flew to

113

the door ahead of me. "You'll love it, Mom!" he promised.

"I'll be right there," I answered. "Why, I wouldn't miss snow on the Chief for all the raspberry whips at the candy store." In spite of my lighthearted reply, my stomach felt nauseous.

Meanwhile, George bounded down the hallway yelling, "Come on, guys! It's the first snow of the year!"

When I arrived at the living room window, they were intently watching each snowflake drift lazily down to join a multitude of white. Joe hung out the dining room window, stretching as far as he could to capture just one flake on a piece of black construction paper.

"Careful, Joe," I warned. "You're going to fall on your head."

"It's okay, Mom," he replied cheerfully. "I already got one!" He slammed the window shut, and the sound reverberated around my head painfully.

Wrapping my arms around George, I said with feeling,"The first snowfall of the year. A very special time for—"

"What's for breakfast, Mom?" George raced off toward the kitchen. "How come I don't smell anything cooking?"

"Because she hasn't started it yet, that's why!" shouted John Jr. from my left elbow. His voice hit my eardrums like a sledge hammer.

"I thought he wanted me to see the snow," I muttered to myself, rubbing my nose with my right wrist. *My nose feels hot*, I thought. Turning so that John Jr. wouldn't see me, I casually brushed my forehead with the back of my hand.

"Got a fever, Mom?" inquired John Jr.

"No!" I snapped back. Why is that kid just like his father? I can't keep *anything* secret!

"Just asking," he responded, hurt. He disappeared downstairs, and I heard him calling, "Specimen! Specimen! Speee-ci-meeennnn!"

If he lets that elephant into the house, I'm going to put that dog up for sale, I promised myself.

Just then George swooped back into the living room—bath towel streaming from his shoulders like a cape. "Like my cape, Mom? I got it tucked in my undershirt. See?" He pointed proudly at his bulging shirt.

"Where are your pajamas?" I tried to keep my head from moving.

"I'm wearing them too," he proudly announced, whipping his cape up so that I could see.

He twirled around the room and glided to a stop next to me. In spite of myself, my heart warmed with love for my freckle-faced boy-wonder.

"How about a hug?" I asked.

"Aw," he replied, arranging his cape, "I'm getting too old to hug a mother."

"Superheroes always treat their mothers with love and tender affection," I answered and grabbed his arm. He wriggled so that all I got was his sleeve. We struggled. By the time I was holding the whole back of his shirt, he had pulled under and out. He squealed with delight at his victory, and I was left holding a pajama top covered with an undershirt and a bath towel. He gave a mighty bounce and zoomed for his room.

"Snow on the Chief means snow for a week," announced Joe seriously, sitting on the sofa.

"Really?" The scuffle with George had left my head feeling lighter than ever, and I answered mechanically, "Where did you hear that?"

"At school." He walked over and stood beside me—another almost-man in the house. "Haven't you ever noticed the Chief, Mom? We live right next to it."

Ignoring his last comment, I asked, "Why will we have snow for a week?"

"Easy." His face came alive with excitement. Joe loved to share knowledge with anyone who would listen. "You simply compute the difference in feet from our elevation to the point of sea level, and then you divide it by—"

"Never mind," I interrupted. "I'll take your word for it." I headed for the kitchen to prepare breakfast.

By mid-afternoon my headache was unbearable, and every bone in my body ached. The boys sat in the middle of the living room rug playing games, and I sat on the sofa holding my head. John Jr. looked up from the checker board, "Mom? Are you feeling okay?"

"Just a little tired," I answered. But I was worried. I couldn't wait for John to arrive home from skiing. I had taken my temperature without the boys knowing, and it was well over 100°. That was two hours ago, and now my head seemed to be floating some distance above my shoulders. My face felt as if it were reflecting dry heat from a fire.

John didn't make it home until after dark. Our only road had been closed because of a minor slide and by the time he walked into the house—cold and weary—I was lying down on the couch.

"Hey, everybody! I'm home," he called as he climbed the stairs.

"Mom's sick!" shouted the boys as they ran from all parts of the house to greet him. "And we're hungry!"

Somehow John organized the boys for hamburgers, soup, and hot chocolate while I gratefully climbed into bed. I didn't wake up till Sunday morning.

I felt too miserable to try to go to church. John and the boys trooped off alone.

Dinner was a disaster, but they struggled on.

Monday morning found Mom still in bed, and no improvement in sight.

When a sore throat developed too, and when I could barely talk, John became concerned.

"I think maybe you should see a doctor," he advised.

"I'll call first thing tomorrow morning," I promised.

Tuesday morning the doctor's receptionist informed me that our doctor would be "away until next Monday. Do you want to leave a message?" An appointment was made for Monday.

I could have seen another doctor, but I didn't like the idea of changing doctors in mid-sickness.

The week passed at a snail's pace, and I staggered around the house, more in the way than anything else. My spirits sagged lower as I saw our home slide from an organized mess to slovenly disorder. I wondered if She had ever really been sick.

Monday finally arrived, and I anxiously dressed for my appointment at 2:00 p.m. Jean arrived at 1:30 to drive me because John didn't think I should drive myself.

We sat in the waiting room for nearly two hours. "It's that

time of year again," the nurse said cheerfully. I didn't answer. I just sagged into the chair and endured.

"Martha?" My doctor's concerned countenance immediately made me feel better. "And what can we do for you today?"

"I'm sick," I began, and listed my symptoms—fever, headache, sore throat, aching limbs, and a light cough. I expected the old "nothing to worry about" routine. Instead he examined me completely and then called me back to his office.

When I'd seated myself across the desk from him, he carefully set down his stethoscope, shuffled through the papers in my file, and lifted a face full of concern. I looked into compassionate gray eyes. "Have you been worried about anything lately?"

"What?" His question caught me off guard.

"Is there anything bothering you? Trouble at home, for example." He folded his hands on top of my file and waited.

"Why, no," I faltered, "I've been having some strange dreams, but . . ." *Had She caused my sickness?* I wondered.

"I didn't think so," he smiled. "But it never hurts to ask." He stood up and handed me a form which he had already filled out. "Take this up to the hospital. We're going to take a few tests."

"What do you think it is?" I knew better than to ask, but it was a reflex action.

"Let's just wait for the test results, shall we?" He patted my shoulder reassuringly and showed me the door.

That night Hampst the Great died. Joe discovered him on the floor of his cage when he went to give him water and food for the night.

From my bed I heard Joe's sobs and John's voice, low and soothing. I lay in bed and cried. Tears for Joe and Hampst and me trickled down my cheeks as I turned in my Bible for comfort. "The Lord gave and the Lord has taken away. Blessed be the name of the Lord."[31] I tried to memorize the verse, but I was so tired that I drifted into an uncomfortable sleep.

A few days later I again sat in my doctor's office, waiting to hear the test results. My doctor swept into the room, pushed his glasses up on his nose, and opened my file.

He didn't hesitate with preliminaries. "The tests show that

your white blood cell count is up. That means infection." He looked gravely at me and delivered his diagnosis, "I believe it's mononucleosis, but I can't be certain at this point."

"The 'kissing disease'?" I was incredulous at the thought. "Only kids get that. Like high school kids . . ." My voice trailed off. I was sure John had not been kissing his students, but must have carried the virus home from school! Visions of our whole family in bed for six weeks made my knees buckle and my head swim. Fortunately I was still sitting down.

"You'll have to go to bed and stay there for the duration," he concluded. "However, it could be just a bad case of flu. We'll just have to wait and see."

Jean drove me home, and I stumbled into the house in a daze. I'd been in bed almost two weeks already. What would happen to the kids? What about John? I knew he was getting tired, trying to be father and mother, teacher and mayor.

Undressing with trembling hands, I decided to take my Bible to bed and read for a while. I read that She also went through periods of privation and sorrow, but her lamp burned continually through the "night of trouble." Lying in bed in the middle of the day, reading my Bible, it suddenly occurred to me that during the winter, nature has its own intent. Some flowers don't bloom brightly unless the winter is hard.

During Her night of trouble, She turned away fear, distrust, and doubt. I wanted to do the same. "At least I can be thankful for a warm bed," I encouraged myself.

"But what will I do for three to six weeks?" Fear stabbed at me. *You will accept My will for you,* a voice seemed to say somewhere inside my soul.

The afternoon dragged as the pain in my body wore at my spirit. Finally I realized that I was like nature. I too needed a winter in my Christian life. Hadn't I asked the Lord to prepare me for His way, the way of the cross?

By the time the kids came home from school, peace had wrapped its gentle mantle around my heart and given me rest. I didn't wake up until dinnertime.

"Supper's on!" John and the boys appeared at my bedroom door carrying a tray with soup and crackers, and a plastic flower in a vase. My eyes filled with tears of gratitude for their love as I pulled myself up to a sitting position.

"Thank you," I replied, while John settled the tray on my lap. John asked the blessing, and then each boy—except George—of his own accord asked God to help me get well.

Later, after the boys were asleep, I explained to John the doctor's verdict. "We'll just have to do as he says," he replied bravely, but I knew it was a blow to him too. He wasn't used to my being out of commission.

"I felt hurt that George didn't pray for me," I confessed.

"He's probably scared about you," John reassured me. "He'll be all right."

The days dragged by. Only those who had been confined to bed can understand the pain of watching life continue for others while it stands still in the sickroom.

George seemed to get quieter with each passing day. I grew concerned about him. No longer bounding from room to room, he withdrew to his room and watched Ben, his guinea pig.

Seven days turned into one week, and still I lay in bed aching. Each time I tried to join the family, I would have to retreat back to bed. My strength was gone. I kept thinking about Her, and Her lamp that didn't go out. I read my Bible and I prayed. "God, help my family. Especially help George. He's too quiet." I had plenty of time to think about life while lying there. I grew increasingly thankful for small joys—sunshine, a warm house, and a loving family.

Still I felt ashamed when I would cry tears of pain and frustration. If I had enough faith, why should I weep? I began to doubt my faith in God, and my suffering began in earnest. Physical pain I could endure, but separation from God—never. The walls of my sickroom closed in on me until finally I cried out to God, "Why?" I knew better than to ask. It was another reflex action.

Her lamp goes not out, but my little light flickered dangerously until I found comfort from my Bible, "Weeping may endure for a night, but joy cometh in the morning."[32]

I realized that my lamp of faith wouldn't go out not because of my own efforts, but because my faith was a gift from God. I felt cleansed, renewed and relieved. I knew I wasn't alone.

That evening when John came to bed, I whispered, "I can accept it now."

"Good," he answered wearily. He fell asleep instantly.

The next morning I felt better. I couldn't explain it, but strength seemed to be flowing into my bones and muscles. I didn't say anything about it, but when they were gone to school, I slowly sneaked to the kitchen to make myself a cup of tea.

By dinnertime I felt hungry—the first time in two weeks. And by evening I managed to sit with the family and listen to their conversation. "Don't do too much too fast, now," warned John.

"I'm fine, really," I replied. And somehow I knew I was.

The next evening I sat on the end of the couch knitting. A fire crackled in the fireplace warming the house against the winter winds. "I think I'm well," I announced happily.

John looked doubtful. John Jr. and Joe continued their checker game, but George leaped up and ran over to me.

"Hooray!" he yelled.

"Sshh," warned John, "your mother—"

"It's fine, really. The noise sounds good!" I smiled at him.

Relief eased the tension lines and the fatigue faded from John's face. "Okay, George. What are you yelling about?"

"Be back in a flash!" He answered, leaping in his superhero-style out of the living room and racing down the hall to his bedroom.

"What do you suppose that's all about?" John asked me, coming over and sitting beside me on the couch.

"I don't know," I answered, puzzled.

George flew back into the living room wearing his cape—the first time since I had become sick. "I just had to check Ben," he announced.

"Why do you keep checking Ben?" I'd noticed him watching his guinea pig often at different times throughout the day.

He hung his head and said nothing. I noticed Joe looking up from his game of checkers. Suddenly George began to cry—great sobs of anguish as though his heart would break.

"What's wrong?" I quickly grabbed him and held him tightly to me.

"Hampst the Great . . ." His muffled words were difficult to understand. "Hampst died, and I thought God took him . . ."

"And you thought God would take Ben too?" John's voice carried deep understanding and sympathy.

George just nodded his head affirmatively. I glanced at Joe and noticed his lip beginning to quiver. "But why did you think that way?" I looked at John Jr. who usually knew everything that went on with his brothers.

John Jr. furrowed his brow and spoke with a steady voice, "Mom, we were all worried about you. We thought"—his voice choked—"that you might . . ." He couldn't continue, and he ducked his head.

Instantly I had my arms wrapped around all three of them, and John tried to hug us at the same time.

The boys began to explain that they had been afraid that I wouldn't get well. They had a meeting in George's room, and decided to offer their pets to God as a sacrifice if He would just make me well. John tried to point out that we no longer offer animals, but they barely heard him.

When Hampst the Great died, they took that as God's judgment. George was waiting for Ben to go next.

John suggested we get a new hamster the very next day. "I'll straighten out their theology later," he whispered to me.

Our trial had changed each of us.

Winter raged outside as a cold wind blew in from the north. But inside our house, warmth radiated from the fireplace, from the love of our children, and from the unfailing love of God. My lamp hadn't gone out.

I wondered if She had ever said, "But He knows the way I take; when He has tried me, I shall come forth as gold."[33]

I was sure that She had.

13 / Friendship

"The heart of her husband trusts in her confidently and relies on and believes in her safely, so that he has no lack of honest gain or need of dishonest spoil."[34]

I approached the meat counter at our local supermarket on Thursday morning with fear coursing through my veins. Remembering all too well the chicken caper—my performance in clearing the chicken counter in less than thirty seconds—shame colored my cheeks bright pink. I recalled how my elbows had flown and my paws had dug madly to grab the most appealing birds in the bunch.

Now I was going to approach the battlefield again. But this time it was going to be different. I was certain of that.

Things had been going quite smoothly for me since my sickness. John had bought a new hamster, Hampst the Second, for Joe. George had stopped watching Ben for signs of God's judgment, and John Jr. had grown another inch.

Indeed, winter is its own time of preparation, I'd philosophized. But as life eased a bit from crisis to comfortable routine, I became bored. With that in mind, I searched the Scripture to see what else She did with Her time.

And that is when I came across the part about Her being a friend to her husband. Speedily looking up "friend" in my concordance, I found this: "Greater love has no one than this, that one lay down his life for his friends."[35]

"That's what John needs," I had encouraged myself. "I will be his friend in need and in deed." I chuckled at my own cleverness in discovering how to be a handy helpmate to my husband. With the wisdom born of hindsight, it is too bad I closed the Book before I read the next verse, "You are My friends, if you do what I command you."[36]

Sitting in my rocking chair, the house to myself, I had reasoned that I would "lay down my life" by giving my dear husband a financial boost. "A penny saved is a penny earned," I hummed to myself while reading all the sales flyers in the newspapers. Feeling a bit wary when I discovered that chickens were to be my savings, I hoped that I would be strong enough not to repeat my previous disaster.

That's when I'd opened my Bible again for a little comfort from Her. My eyes spied a passage that I'd always missed before. "Her husband is known in the city's gates, where he sits among the elders of the land."[37] (I should have quit while I was ahead.)

"Just like John!" I'd exclaimed. At that moment I lost my bit of modesty, replacing humility with hypocrisy.

"I am a mayor's wife," I recited to myself as I walked into the grocery store. "Therefore I will behave with proper dignity." Head held high, nose pointed upward, I knew that She could not have walked down the aisle toward the meat counter any more royally than I did. She wouldn't have done what I was about to do. (She probably wished that *I* had never heard of *Her*.)

As I grabbed a cart, I muttered to myself, "John will never need to moonlight. Not while I'm around to help." I swooped toward the poultry section.

I breathed a sigh of gratitude for my strength under stress as I arranged only three pink and white chickens neatly in the bottom of my grocery cart.

"Ah, the sweet taste of victory," I murmured softly as I swung away from my previous undoing. *I will become like Her, and John will be thankful for me,* I reasoned as I walked slowly down the aisle.

And then I saw it. Glued to the spot, I stared at the sign. It shouted at me: BACON! SO CHEAP IT'S ALMOST FREE! *Free,*

free, free! spun around in my head. Reeling, I recalled my friend telling me about my previous shopping frenzy, "You took the best ten pounds of bacon with one swipe of your hand. . . ."

I blinked to clear my vision. The sign actually said: Bacon—Reduced: Buy NOW and SAVE.

"Caught you this time, Greed—you enemy of my soul's peace." I spoke out loud to the temptation.

"Did you want some help?" offered a passing clerk. She smiled slightly as she waited for me to reply.

"No, thank you," I answered, flushing.

The placard was printed in fire-engine red letters. *Red is the color that incites one to riot. I should have known,* I thought.

I knew She would be proud of me as I demurely picked up two pounds of bacon from the top of the pile.

"Fancy meeting you here!" A voice broke my concentration.

"Why, hello there! How wonderful to see you again!" I couldn't remember her at all, except for a vague feeling of dislike. Was it her fault or mine? Was a "social lie" acceptable in this case?

We stood in the center of the grocery store aisle and renewed our previous surface relationship—or lack of it, I felt. And I played right along with the game.

In the final analysis, I had replaced greed with dishonesty, but I didn't care. I was eager to see if she noticed any difference in me. I eventually recalled I had met her at a church function a couple of years earlier. She and her husband wanted children but didn't have any. That was about all I could recall about her situation, but I expected her to notice my Christian growth in fullest detail.

She prattled on about her family history and how she and her huband had been blessed with triplets. She wound up with, ". . . and so we decided to move back here."

As soon as she paused, I tuned in again. It was my turn. "We're so glad to have you back." I stretched the truth just a shade. "My husband, John, the *mayor*, should declare a day of homecoming just for you two!" I couldn't believe my own ears at my pretense.

She totally missed the importance of John's position. "Isn't this a wonderful day?" she bubbled on. Her eyes sparkled like her tone of voice.

I excused myself at the first break in her conversation. I was coming unglued. "I'm really very busy today," I interjected, though I was really not, "and I'm finished with my shopping (another untruth). I will see you another time." I practically crawled to the check-out counter.

My face blushed with shame and humiliation as I walked from the grocery store to the post office. But by the time I had purchased stamps and complimented myself for walking to achieve physical fitness, my remorse had turned into confidence. *After all*, I reasoned, *I really had done well in facing down that sale sign—what are a few little white lies among friends?* My mind soothed my ruffled spirit.

By the time I pulled into the driveway, I was cheerful again. I gazed through the windshield at the Chief for a moment. "Chief, I'm taking the day off!" I announced. I turned my head backwards and aimed for the road.

"What I need is some company. Wonder what Jean is doing?" I drove straight to Jean's house.

Roaring into the driveway and screeching to a halt, I jumped out of the car and bounded onto her front porch. I peered in the porch window and spied her standing at the kitchen sink. *Probably washing dishes*, I guessed, and rapped on the windowpane to get her attention.

She smiled and waved for me to enter. Ignoring her barking Chihuahuas, I waltzed into the kitchen and sat down at the table.

"How 'bout a cup of coffee?" she inquired as she filled a mug.

"Great!" My tone was too light.

"What's wrong?" she asked casually.

"Whatever do you mean?" I evaded her question and smiled brightly as I threw my jacket over the back of another chair.

"Just asking," she responded, pouring herself a cup of hot coffee and seating herself across the table from me.

"Do you know what friends are for?" I changed the subject.

"No, what are friends for?" She played along with me, amused.

"Well, I was thinking about it on the way over here, and I

decided that true friendship is based on sacrifice." I blew on my coffee for emphasis.

"Sacrifice? What makes you think that?" She'd suffered through my explanations other times, and I could see her settling in to endure my latest idea.

"You're a good example," I replied. "You're going to listen, and that's a sacrifice."

"I don't have a choice," she chuckled.

"That's right, you don't," I replied seriously. "That's what makes a friendship work."

She nodded sympathetically.

"Remember the time I was sick and you took all the kids to the zoo?" I sipped my coffee, waiting for her response.

"Anyone would have done that," she answered, staring intently at me.

"What's bothering me is that I've been telling lies lately." I blurted it out in one breath.

"Lies?" she gently inquired.

"I don't know what is wrong with me." I plunged right into the problem before I had time to change my mind. "I went to the grocery store with the idea that I could save money for John, sale shop, and yet not go crazy and grab everything in sight."

"That's good!" she encouraged.

"That part was okay until I started telling somebody—I can't remember her name—that I was thrilled to see her again, when I wasn't . . ." I hung my head in shame.

"Oh," she nodded her head in understanding. But I knew Jean couldn't really help me because she didn't know about Her.

"Maybe you're trying too hard," she soothed. "You did resist the impulse to clean out the sale counters, didn't you?"

"Thanks." I covered my disappointment in her answer. "That helps a lot." I stood up and reached for my jacket. "Well," I went on with my prevarications, "I've got a sink full of dirty dishes. Guess I'd best get home and get to work."

My isolation was complete. I arrived home with a sore spirit and a weary heart. Instead of hoarding chickens in the deep freeze, I stored lies in my unclean heart. And I was going to be John's best friend.

A tear trickled out of my left eye as I slowly climbed the stairs to the kitchen. *No dishes*, my mind accused. Unable to stand any more mental strain, I trudged to the rocker and caved in.

Creak, creak, creak, "I'll get my Bible," I announced to myself and hurried to its place on my night table. "Obviously I'm doing something wrong," I muttered, taking the Bible back to the rocking chair with me. "God, what am I doing wrong?" It was the first time I had asked God to help since the beginning of the day, several hours earlier.

I reread the part I'd marked earlier about laying down one's life for a friend. "What's this?" I questioned in surprise: ". . . if you do what I command you."

Suddenly the cobwebs cleared from my eyes. I could see clearly what I had done. In my efforts to be the ideal friend to my husband on my own strength, I had ignored the fact that God's power comes to us only through obedience to His Word.

"Why, I never even asked John what he thought!" I sat in shock at my discovery. I knew that I was to follow his leadership—even though many of my friends disagreed with that part of the Bible—not for his sake alone, but for my protection and safety as well.

Remorse filled my heart. Perhaps John didn't want me to be money-grubbing at the supermarket. "It probably makes him feel good to know that he provides well for us," I said to myself with deep sincerity.

Flipping the pages of my Bible to Proverbs, a verse almost jumped at me, "A man of many friends comes to ruin, but there is a friend who sticks closer than a brother."[38] I found another scripture that made sense to me too, "A friend loves at all times, and a brother is born for adversity."[39]

I sat and reflected as peace filled my soul for the first time that day. Suddenly it all came together. *She* knew how to honor her husband as She also knew how to honor Christ by obeying His commands.

"I'm sorry, Lord. I've been on the wrong track again. Please help me. I want to learn."

Those scriptures shed light on the whole subject and gave me the way to follow. I would lay down my life for my husband by obeying God's command to follow his leadership in our home. I usually did as I pleased and expected him to approve of me just as I was. I knew he didn't want to tyrannize me, and he really didn't expect me to follow him blindly. But what a gift of love and real friendship it would be if I simply took my place beside him—instead of running out in front.

In the quiet moments that followed, God revealed much about me and Her. "A virtuous and worthy wife—earnest and strong in character—is a crowning joy to her husband."[40]

I liked that. I wanted to be a crowning joy to John.

"But woman is [the expression of] man's glory."[41]

Right there in my living room as I rocked back and forth, I made up my mind to be a better wife. From now on I would ask John what he thought about things instead of just expecting him to rubber stamp my decisions. And I would have to really work on this lying business.

But the first thing I'm going to do is to finish the grocery shopping, I decided.

"I've been behaving like a raving maniac all day," I said, grabbing the car keys.

I flew past the meat counter with nary a glance at a chicken, grabbed some milk, cheese and some laundry detergent. "I know, I'll make steamed broccoli for dinner."

I confidently wheeled my cart to the produce section. I was not prepared for the tomato sale.

HOT HOUSE TOMATOES! CHEAP! CHEAP! CHEAP! The sign looked as if it were billboard size.

Pure red ambrosia beckoned to me as I envisioned tomato juice, quarts of home-canned tomatoes lining my pantry shelves, oodles of sliced tomatoes on crisp beds of green lettuce. My mouth watered as I plunged my hands into the pile of crimson "love apples."

"Ah, juicy, red, ripe, meaty, firm," I warbled as I piled my shopping cart high with bags of tomatoes. A lady to my left with gray hair was wearing a worried expression.

Turning to face her, I enthusiastically inquired, "Wanna know where they hide the best ones?"

"What's that?" She raised her eyebrows in surprise.

I leaned closer, stretching across the counter. "See," I explained, picking out a juicy, ripe tomato, "they always put the old ones in the front."

"Oh," she replied as though humoring a lunatic. "I—I see."

I stuffed a couple more in a sack and pressed the package into her hands.

Stunned, she stood holding the bag, and I sailed serenely out of the store exulting. "In the sea of life I will ride the waves to victory!"

Like a ship off course, I was drifting, barely hours away from my most recent resolve, toward disaster. Although my head contained all the knowledge necessary to emulate Her behavior, my heart was at sea.

14 / Christmas

"Strength and dignity are her clothing, and her position is strong and secure. She rejoices over the future—the latter day or time to come [knowing that she and her family are in readiness for it]!"[42]

Humming "Away in a Manger," I poked a brown raisin into the tummy of another gingerbread boy. I was ready to pop him into the oven.

"You are cute, cute, cute," I said. Gingerbread boys held a special fascination for me. So I made an army of them every Christmas. Soft, puffy lads would greet our boys from the mantle, the tree, and the table.

Cookie men had enthralled me since early childhood, ever since I'd first heard the story about the gingerbread boy who ran away from a farmer's wife. I felt awful about his being tricked and gobbled up by the wolf. So as soon as I was old enough, I began to create all kinds of cookie people who would be safe from wolves.

Humming at the kitchen counter, I admired the gingerbread boy I was about to bake. With a citron bow tie, a cherry mouth, and raisin buttons, he looked like he had leaped from a page in a picture book.

"Fee, fie, fo, fum. I can't wait for cinnamon!" shouted George when he saw me gathering cookbooks for Christmas baking.

"It's *ginger*, stupid," corrected Joe ungraciously.

"Make tons," John Jr. interjected. "And put lots of that white frosting I like on them," he added.

I began my Christmas baking in November, just after buying all those tomatoes.

I'd felt unsettled since that day in the supermarket, but I didn't know why. I was back to disliking Her intensely, which bothered me. I hoped that baking would be a positive pursuit.

"Work is therapeutic," I comforted myself as I began my task with great vigor. After five Christmas cakes, fourteen types of fancy cookies, and fudge and divinity, I decided that gingerbread boys needed a gingerbread house.

What a house! Two feet tall, one foot wide, it took more flour and sugar than all of the other baking put together. "They'll love it!" I exclaimed as I piled on white fluffy icing and stuck peppermint patties all over the roof. I completed the picture with tiny elves perched on the gumdrop chimney and Mrs. Santa Claus on the second floor.

"*She* never made a house like this—even in heaven!" I pronounced as I hefted the huge house onto a large piece of pressed board covered with aluminum foil. I basked in the praise of my family.

"Mmmm," said George as his eyes widened at the sight.

"When do we get to eat it?" inquired practical John Jr.

"It sure is big!" exclaimed Joe.

"A little large, don't you think?" commented John.

"No, it is not 'a little large,' " I retorted. And I stomped back out to the kitchen to bake Christmas breads from different countries of the world.

I'd probably made enough food to feed the world. If not, I was about to create a flour famine.

By the second week in December, the freezer was full to the brim with sumptuous goodies. I also noted with satisfaction my pantry shelves which were lined with home-canned juice and stewed tomatoes.

"Deck my shelves with lots of goodies . . . fa, la, la, la, la, la, la, la, la," I sang as I tripped up and down the stairs bearing the fruits of my ambition.

When the Saturday before Christmas Eve arrived, I stepped up production.

"Come on and help me beat this fudge, boys," I called.

They were never far from the sound of my voice during my baking marathon—especially since they were out of school for the holidays. Three boys followed their noses to the kitchen.

"Yum!" exclaimed George as he eyed the bubbling candy on the stove.

"When do we get to eat it?" asked John Jr. as usual.

"You have to beat it first, dummy," retorted Joe.

"I'll beat your nose over to the other side of your face!" threatened the elder brother, raising his fists and dancing around the kitchen like a heavyweight boxing champion.

"Says who!" Joe sneered.

"Cut it out!" I shouted above the din.

"Says me! That's who!" growled John Jr., giving Joe a push. The dog chose that moment to move to a new location. Joe tripped over him, hit the handle of the candy pan, and boiling candy tipped over and poured onto my right foot. I screamed.

"Mom's hurt!" yelled George, running pell-mell to find his dad.

Two hours later—after a trip to the emergency ward—I lay flat on my back on the sofa, staring at the ceiling.

"Can I get you anything, Mom?" begged John Jr.

"Don't speak to me." I winced in pain.

"Maybe a cup of tea?" inquired Joe.

"Don't you *dare* come near me with anything hot!" I shrieked.

"Mom?" The face of George pushed through to peer into my face.

"Yes?" He was the only one I could currently tolerate in the same room with me. I was afraid that if I spoke to either one of the others before I'd cooled off, it would destroy them forever.

"I just wondered if we're still going to have Christmas now that you can't walk very well." A tear brimmed in each eye and glistened behind his glasses.

"Just let me rest now, please," I replied painfully. "Yes, we'll have Christmas," I relented when I saw the trembling lip. "Where is your father?"

"He went downtown to do some shopping. He said that since you were okay now, we could take care of you until he gets back."

"Oh," I responded without expression. The initial concern from the boys soon wore off, and by the time John had returned from his shopping, I was fit to be tied. The boys had done nothing except fight, make noise, and chase the dog. The hamster was loose somewhere in the house, and Ben, according to George, had caught a cold; "Will he die?"

On the following Saturday, Christmas Eve, my foot felt better. My emotions did not.

That's when the flood hit.

I should have realized the weather was acting strangely for the Christmas season, but I was mostly preoccupied with myself and my injury. John noticed, however, and he had been worried. That's where he'd been after I'd burned my foot. Instead of shopping, he had called an emergency meeting of the town council to discuss the lack of diking in our town.

The council agreed that the best we could hope for this year was colder weather. A snow-melt up high, coupled with a heavy rainfall, could spell flood conditions for our area, since we lived in a valley. Especially dangerous was an old dam which had threatened to give way the year before. It could allow tons of water to rush unchecked right down the main street of town.

I was hobbling around the kitchen preparing a turkey to cook for Christmas Day. I peered out the kitchen window to look for the boys who had been playing football in a nearby vacant lot. "The wind is really whipping!" I exclaimed to myself.

At dinnertime, John seemed unusually quiet.

"Anything wrong?" I asked.

"The weather has me a bit concerned, that's all. Nothing to worry about though," he said lightly and cuffed George playfully on the chin.

As we ate, I could hear the rain pelting on the rooftop and the wind howling around the house.

I was in the middle of serving dessert when I heard some unusual sounds from outside. Fear immediately gripped me.

Trying to cover my panic, I casually inquired of John, "Do you hear that?"

"It's the river," he replied seriously. "The current is becoming so strong that it's disturbing the riverbed." He rose from the table and walked toward the telephone in the kitchen. "I'd better call a quick meeting to see what we're going to do about it."

I heard him talking in a low tone, and then he returned to the table. "What is it?" I asked in a worried voice.

He calmly gazed at his three sons and me. "Why don't you finish your dessert now," he smiled reassuringly at the boys. Then, "Martha, I'd like a quick word with you."

"Sure," I agreed as terror crawled up my spine. I followed him to our bedroom. "What is it, John?" Dread pushed all other emotion out of my consciousness.

"Flood," John said quietly.

"Here?" I couldn't believe my ears. Floods happened to other people, not to us.

"Now, listen carefully," he continued. "You may have to evacuate—"

"Me? Us? Where will *you* be?" Apprehension at having to face a crisis without John caused my knees to turn to water.

"Don't worry, Martha." He was already grabbing his car keys from the dresser. "You can do it."

"Where will you *be*?" I repeated while numbness spread through me.

"Martha!" John squeezed my shoulders hard. "Get a hold of yourself. Where is your faith?" He relaxed his grip and continued in a reproving voice, "Somebody has to go, and I don't need to have you to worry about too. You'll be fine."

His last phrase echoed in my brain as he spoke quietly to each of the boys. A horn honked outside in the blackness, and he was gone. *You'll be fine*—hadn't I heard that somewhere? Then I remembered. Viv had told me I would be fine when I began sewing my blouse. "My blouse wasn't fine. My blouse was horrible," I whispered to myself.

Mechanically I did as John had instructed. We finished dessert, and I tried to appear unafraid as the boys and I cleaned up the table and washed the dishes. "We won't use the dishwasher," I advised. I didn't have any reason, except that doing dishes would keep us all busy.

"Listen, guys!" shouted Joe in excitement. He ran to the living room window and opened it wide. A torrent of rain blew in, and the noise of the river sounded like the Chief beginning to crumble.

"Close that window!" I commanded.

Six eyes bored into mine and read my alarm. Joe closed the window without argument.

"Now listen, kids," I began, "I don't want to worry you, but Dad says there may be a flood—"

"A flood? Hooray!" whooped George. "Just like on television!" He began to race around the room.

"Hampst!" shrieked Joe. "Where is Hampst?" Terror filled his eyes as he began a frantic search around the room.

John Jr. stared at me, his blue eyes clear, and asked, "Did Dad say anything about Specimen?"

"Maybe you should call her in," I replied, feeling faint. "Excuse me for a minute, will you?" I fled to our bedroom, closed the door, and fell on my knees. "Help me, God," I prayed, "I'm *so* afraid."

Right in the middle of the storm, I reached for my Bible. And while terror shook my body, alone with God, I read His Word and was comforted. "Bid the older women . . . to give good counsel. . . . They will wisely train the young women to be . . . self-controlled . . . subordinating themselves to their husbands, that the word of God may not be exposed to reproach—blasphemed or discredited."[43]

"You'll be fine," I could almost hear John's voice. I rose from my knees and headed for the living room.

"Have you found Hampst yet?" My calm voice sounded foreign to my ears. George sensed a difference too. I could tell from his answer.

"Joe isn't here, Mom. He went to his room." He came over and wrapped his arms around my waist. "You look brave too. Just like Daddy."

"Good," I said, giving him a bear hug. "Now, how about getting Ben ready to travel?"

"We goin' somewhere? Great!" His eyes flashed with excitement. "I'll get *lots* of carrots for Ben! Enough for a whole week!" He ran to the kitchen, and I heard the fridge door opening and carrots being dumped on the floor. For once I didn't care about the amount.

"Oh, for the faith of a child," I said softly as I headed for Joe's room. I had a feeling he would be there, trying to hide his fear about Hampst the Second being lost.

Opening the door a crack, I called, "Joe?"

"Come on in, Mom," came a discouraged voice.

He sat on the edge of his bed with his head in his hands. "Did you find Hampst?" I asked gently, sure that he hadn't.

"Oh, Mom!" Tears of anguish coursed down his cheeks, and my heart suffered with him for his loss. I hugged him tightly and felt his misery.

Smoothing his hair with my hand, I suggested, "You know, Joe, God loves Hampst too. Did you ever think about asking Him to help us find Hampst?"

Joe looked up at me, hope lighting his brown eyes. "Could we?" He wiped his tears with his shirt-sleeves.

Together we prayed about Hampst the Second. Then I said, "Now you go and look for him, and we'll leave the results to God."

"Okay, Mom," he replied, and he was off like a shot, calling "Hampst! Here boy! Hampst!"

John Jr. returned from the basement. He was soaking wet and covered with mud. "I found Specimen," he announced proudly. "I've got her tied up in the basement."

"Excellent!" I commended him for his responsible behavior. "Now, how about you changing into some dry clothes?"

"Okay!" he exclaimed, beaming. "Anything else?"

"Yes, there is something more for you to do. Dad said we may have to evacuate—"

"You mean leave the house?" his eyes widened in surprise.

"Yes." I continued calmly, "I need you to collect our sleeping bags, a couple of Bibles, and whatever else you think we might need for an overnight stay." I paused to take a deep breath. "Do you think you can handle it?" I patted him on the shoulder. He seemed inches taller than he had an hour earlier.

"You bet!" he replied, racing off on his mission.

"So far, so good. Thanks, Lord," I whispered. I stood in the hall for a moment, wondering what to do next. A strange urge to walk into the living room hit me, and without thinking, I strolled slowly into the room. Something scurried along the edge of the couch—one tiny, brown ball of fluff propelled by four pink feet. "Hampst!" I exclaimed softly. "Joe! Come quickly!"

In a second Joe stood at the other end of the couch. "Hampst!"

Five minutes later, Hampst the Second sat munching sunflower seeds, safe in his cage. "Thanks again, God!" I said softly as I began to prepare some sandwiches and a thermos of hot chocolate.

One by one the boys popped into the kitchen. "Hampst is ready to travel," announced Joe happily.

"Specimen is waiting. And I got a bag of dog food for her," said John Jr.

"Ben has enough carrots for about a month!" George flitted from the step stool to the stove in eager anticipation.

"Good," I replied, finishing the sandwiches. "Now, how would you like to get me the picnic hamper?"

Three boys shot down the stairs and reappeared in minutes bearing the insulated case, three bags of marshmallows and some potato chips. The disaster had taken on the air of a picnic outing as they scurried to gather some candles and matches.

What a Christmas Eve, I thought as I tidied the kitchen and packed the rest of the food in the hamper. "Better turn off the lights on the Christmas tree and unplug the television," I ordered.

We had just finished our preparations when the noise of the boulders bumping in the rushing river could no longer be ignored. Alarmed, I spoke quietly to the boys, "I think I'll just take a quick look out front. I'll be right back." Descending the stairs to the front door, I looked outside. Our maple tree bent in the wind almost to the ground, and leaves and sticks whirled everywhere. "I wonder if we're supposed to leave?" I asked myself. Suddenly I felt we should go. Quickly climbing the stairs, I called, "Boys, turn off the lights in your rooms. I think we'll leave now."

I was surprised at how well the boys handled themselves as we loaded the car, the dog, the guinea pig, and Hampst the Second.

Just as I was backing the car out of the driveway, the river jumped its banks. A wall of water hurtled down the street to-ward us. As I floored the accelerator, the water was already sweeping away lawns and driveways.

"Just like the Indianapolis 500!" yelled George as I squealed the tires and the car lurched forward.

It was the wildest ride of my life. We hit the bottom of the hill just before the water in a tiny rivulet exploded over the sides of the road and buried it in mud. And we reached the top of the hill just before lightning dropped a telephone pole across the intersection leading into town.

Police officers met us at every point. They were carrying radio receivers, and we could hear the crackle of voices on the short-waves as they waved us on toward the elementary school in the center of town. "How brave they are!" I exclaimed. They stood without protection in the middle of the storm, directing others toward safety.

At two o'clock on Christmas morning, most of the residents were in safe areas. I still hadn't seen John, but I heard that he was out along the riverbanks with other men, checking the rising water level. I prayed that God would keep him and the others safe.

At 3:00 a.m., the boys finally slept on the gymnasium floor beside me. All around us were others who had been forced to leave their homes to the mercy of the flood.

Unknown to me, John and some other men had gone to check the old dam high above the town. If that gave way, tons of water would cover the whole valley as it had early in the century, with terrible loss of life.

Sitting on the school gym floor, I prayed for the safety of our town. I knew nothing about the disaster which threatened, but I did know that Christmas Day two thousand years ago, God poured out His love on mankind. I asked Him to save us all this Christmas Day. Tears glistened, then dripped to the floor. I sat with my head on my knees interceding for friends and strangers. I left the results with God.

At 5:00 a.m. I was in the arms of my husband. He had returned to find us huddled in the school gymnasium. "Oh, John! I'm so thankful you're safe," I whispered as I hugged him.

He said nothing, but the expression of his face told me more than a thousand words. He was tired, but pleased that the threat was over. "The water has begun to recede," he said simply.

"How long will we have to stay here?" I asked him.

Putting his arm around my shoulder, he answered, "There may be another storm on the way."

"We will be fine," I said with conviction.

John remembered his earlier remark and his rebuke. His eyes softened. Looking deep into my eyes, he whispered, "Merry Christmas, Excellent Wife."

From him it was a compliment of the highest order. I recalled another verse I'd read while kneeling in terror in our bedroom: "Guide the household, [and] not give opponents of the faith occasion for slander or reproach."[44]

A wave of love for my husband swept over me, followed by overwhelming gratitude to God for the tiny baby Jesus, who had graced a manger and changed the course of mankind. Squeezing John's hands tightly, I replied simply, "Thank you."

15 / *Thanks*

"She makes for herself coverlets, cushions and . . . her clothing is of linen, pure white and fine."[45]

"Oh, John, I can't believe it!" I exclaimed when we arrived back home late Christmas Day. Although the front yard was covered with mud and the driveway broken and buried by the ravaging river, our house was untouched.

"Look, Dad!" George shouted from the back seat of the car. "The water went almost to the house, and then it stopped!"

"Just like the Red Sea," murmured Joe in awe.

"Almost," John replied, giving me a wink, "but not quite."

"When may we open our presents?" inquired ever-practical John Jr.

"As soon as *you* sweep up the yard," John replied solemnly.

"And," I added, "repair the driveway." I laughed when I saw my oldest son's face fall, then light up as soon as he realized we were only kidding.

"So give me a shovel!" he yelled in my left ear.

"Everybody out!" John instructed.

As soon as we had emptied the automobile, carried in our belongings, and returned the pets to their respective stations— backyard, front room (small cage), and George's room (big cage)— we assembled in front of the Christmas tree.

"May I turn on the lights?" asked George.

John nodded his head affirmatively, and we were silent as

145

the tree lit up and glowed before us. A special blue bulb hung over the manger scene beneath the decorated fir, giving an air of nighttime to the creche.

"Are we going to read the Christmas story?" John Jr. inquired.

"You bet we are," answered John, nodding to me.

"Get the Bible, Joe," I said.

Joe raced to get the old Bible which had been passed down in our family for generations. He handed it to John and sat down on the floor next to me.

"And it came to pass in those days . . ." John's deep voice seemed to sweep away the cares of the past days and return me to the stable in Bethlehem where Jesus lay sleeping. Gratitude filled me as I sat there surrounded by my family. I silently prayed for those whose homes were not left untouched by the flood.

Later, when we sat surrounded by tissue paper and Christmas wrap, the inevitable question came from John Jr. "Dad, may we set up the electric train you and Mom gave us?" He chose his words carefully.

"Of course," replied John casually. And then he reclined on the sofa with a magazine. Six stricken eyes bored into mine. I knew what they wanted, but then, so did John. I decided not to interfere.

The boys stood silently in the middle of the living room.

John glanced up from his reading. "Oh," he teased, "you mean *now*?" He gave me a wink.

"It's pretty late, don't you think? What about your bedtime?" he continued.

"Could we just lay out the track?" coaxed John Jr., the self-appointed spokesman.

"We can't stay up *all* night," responded John, "but if you want to get your pajamas on—"

Like a shot, three boys bolted for their rooms.

"If only they would behave like that all year," I sighed as I sat down next to John on the couch.

Within minutes they had returned—pajamas on, hair combed, blue goo on the chin of the youngest.

John threw himself into the project, and by four o'clock in

the morning, the track of the miniature railroad was laid. It had been a tough job. First, cork soaked in warm water for flexibility was glued to the plywood board. Then tiny spikes were driven through tiny holes in the track which had been laid on the cork roadbed.

"Oh," John groaned, straightening, "my back is killing me. How about a cup of coffee?"

"Certainly," I replied, and hurried to the kitchen.

At 6:00 in the morning, after staying up all night, we drank coffee and ate gingerbread boys and grapefruit. George, however, lay asleep in the corner of the living room, snuggled in his new comforter.

By 8:00 the remaining "engineers" lay asleep, too.

Dad had been bitten by the "railroad fever," so by two o'clock he and the boys were back at work, bent over the layout in the center of the living room rug.

I, on the other hand, had a project of my own to begin. My dearest friend, Jean, had given me a kit, complete with yarn and fabric, for making cushions and an afghan. While the men labored on the floor, I sat on the end of the sofa surrounded by scissors, patterns and needles of all sizes. I enjoyed listening to the comments of the railroad crew . . .

"I thought we weren't going to stay up all night," commented John Jr.

"Here, hold this," commanded Dad.

"Maybe next year the whole track can light up," Joe suggested.

"Now, here's a house for you, a store for you, and a cottage for you," continued Father.

"A train doesn't need lights to see where it's going, stupid," retorted John Jr. to Joe.

"Doesn't a train have to have light?" whined Joe.

"Here's some glue for you," muttered John in deep concentration. Handing the small tube to George, he seemed unaware of any conflict.

By Monday evening, the day after Christmas, John was landscaping the layout, while the boys were watching television, and I was cutting out patches for quilt pillows.

Peace reigned during that Christmas holiday in spite of the flood.

However, as often happens in moments of relative tranquillity, the tiny bug of self-sufficiency had bitten my Achilles' tendon. While I sat on the couch, knitting, I had time to observe my husband in action and found His Christian life lacking a bit. It wasn't anything he *did* in particular. But as I compared him to great evangelists, noted martyrs and missionaries, he seemed to need a bit of a boost.

It all began innocently enough when I said, "Maybe I can't sew, but I'm going great guns on cushions and afghans!" I waited for his loving response.

"I said I'm really getting good at this. I guess it doesn't matter that I can't sew." I stared at John who was hunched over the railroad checking wires.

"Hold that, Joe," he said.

"Did you hear me, John?" I sang sweetly.

John raised his eyes in my direction, and I noticed his glazed expression.

Why, he LOVES working on that train! I thought. The rest of the accusations that paraded through my brain at that moment are unspeakable. Suffice it to say that I felt shut out by a toy railroad. I became angry.

John finally replied, "Uh, huh. Yeah." He didn't realize his delayed response was worse than no response.

As I sat cutting and crocheting, my mind raced around at lightning speed. John lacked the gift of love for his wife. After all, he failed to appreciate my talents and efforts. He didn't even thank me for my delicious Christmas dinner. John, therefore, needed a boost in his Christian life.

I decided that behind every good man a good woman pushes and shoves. I didn't bother to think whether or not *She* would have reformed her husband's spiritual life. *I will teach him gently,* was my righteous thought.

I'd taken a huge bite out of an unsightly apple.

The first day of school after Christmas vacation, I marched straight to the local Christian bookstore. I purchased several books on husbands loving their wives as Christ loved His church, a few tracts, and a cross on a chain. I noticed how spiritual the men who wore crosses seemed to be and found my husband lacking by comparison. (Why, my John hardly ever said "Praise the Lord!" when he stubbed his toe on a bookshelf.)

That Monday evening, after all the kids were in bed, I presented him with my present. "I bought something for you today," I said with loving smotheringness.

John's eyes lighted up. "You did? But Christmas is over." He seemed happy with my surprise as he opened the small box.

I waited in anticipation for his approval of my choice.

John opened a velvet-covered case and lifted out a two-inch wooden cross suspended by a heavy stainless steel chain.

I smiled brightly in anticipation of his reaction.

"It's very nice," he said, as he replaced the cross in the box.

"Aren't you going to wear it?" I couldn't wait to see how it looked.

"Little late now, don't you think?" He patted my shoulder. "I can wear it tomorrow." Then he climbed into bed and instantly fell asleep.

Tuesday morning, undaunted, I was up and dressed before breakfast.

The family appeared, ate, and left. John offered to drive the kids to school for me.

"Oh, well," I muttered to myself, digging out tracts from my supply sack which I'd stashed in the hall closet. "I'll just put a few of these around the house. It probably will take some time to get him going."

I deposited a few in the bathroom, placed some on the coffee table in the living room, and (giggle) hid about ten of them all over his desk in his study. He'd be certain to find them as soon as he went to work on his thesis that evening.

Now, what? I wondered. Laying my finger on the side of my nose, up out of the rocking chair I rose. "I've got it!" I exclaimed, hurrying to find a pencil and paper. "A wife should be a good helper, and I'm going to help. Just wait until he sees this!"

Gathering pens, paper, and ruler, I seated myself at the kitchen table. Meticulously I wrote at the top of the blank page, "Long (and Short) Range Plan for the Christian life."

I labored at my task all morning, and by lunchtime I gazed at my posters with satisfaction. *Ah, yes,* I said to myself, *it's all there—charts, diagrams, shepherds, and a baby lamb.* I hoped that John would see himself as the lamb learning to find its way in the maze of Christianity.

As soon as the boys arrived for lunch, I fed them peanut butter sandwiches and apples. No muss; no fuss. When I had shooed them back to school, I threw away the paper towels on which I'd served their sandwiches, and dived into hanging my freshly created posters.

"This is better than Christmas!" I exclaimed to the Chief as I flew past the living room window.

Wisely, the Chief remained silent.

Exhausted from my efforts, I lay down on the sofa for a quick nap.

"What'cha doin' asleep, Mom?" George's nose was bumping my beak.

"What?" I bolted upright. "What are you doing here?"

"School is out," he replied nervously, shuffling his feet. "Did you have another dream?"

"Of course not," I answered quickly.

"Then what are you doing lying down?" He squinted his eyes in suspicion.

"Nothing," I retorted, rising from the couch. "I'm going to fix dinner now."

As I left the room, I thought I heard him mutter, "Women!" I decided to let it pass.

"Hi, Mom," mumbled Joe as he went down the hall to his room.

"How was school?" I hollered after him.

"I hate school!" he shouted just before he slammed the door to his room.

"Hey, Mom?" John Jr.'s voice filtered up from the basement. "Did you let Specimen loose?"

"Isn't she tied up?" I called down the steps to the worried voice of my oldest son. I tried to recall when I'd last seen the dog. "You'd better go and look for her." I remembered the last time Specimen had run through the neighborhood. By the time she arrived back home, she was wearing a garden fence; six people were chasing her, throwing sticks. As a result my neighbors didn't speak to me for a long time. . . .

Putting the macaroni and wieners on to simmer until time to eat, I hurried outside to help John Jr. hunt him down.

No sooner had I yelled, "Spehh-ci-muuun!" than John pulled into the driveway.

"Hi, sweetie," I crooned, planting a huge kiss upon his right cheek.

Startled, he appeared uncomfortable. "Uh, huh . . ." he replied.

"Is that all you can say after all I've done for you today?" I stomped toward the house.

John, puzzled by my erratic behavior, picked up his briefcase and some books. "I've got work to do in my study," he mumbled as he disappeared.

Hurrying back into the house after him, I went straight to the hall closet and pulled out the two GOD LOVES YOU! bumper stickers I'd purchased for the car as another surprise for John.

"This will help him to be a better witness," I muttered to myself as I carefully unrolled one of the fluorescent, fuchsia-colored signs. "Lovely!" I whispered excitedly.

"I'll be outside, John!" I yelled as I ran out the door.

"I think I'll do the front bumper first. What do you think?" I asked the hood of the car. Squatting down on my heels, I carefully peeled off the backing and applied the sign.

"Oh, dear," I said, "it's crooked." *Never mind*, I soothed inwardly.

Walking around the car to the rear bumper, I unrolled the second sign. My eyes widened in surprise. "How did I get this one?" The sticker read: PREPARE TO MEET YOUR MAKER! It was all decorated with planets and swirling galaxies in various shades of brilliant yellow and bright green. "Humm," I said, applying the poster to the bumper, "this one should really have gone on the front." *Never mind*.

Having completed that little job, I called the family to the table for dinner.

Joe was still grouchy as he stuffed huge amounts of macaroni noodles into his mouth.

"Don't bolt your food, Joe," I ordered.

"Mumph, gumfph, gulp," responded Joe.

"I can't find Specimen." John Jr. looked down at his plate.

"Maybe he died?" George paused in mid-bite. "Maybe—"

"Never mind," John said to George. "She'll come back, Johnny. Don't worry."

Three days later we still had no information about the elephant-dog. John hadn't commented on the bumper stickers, *or* the tracts, *or* the posters which depicted Christian growth in six easy steps. He did, however, read the newspaper a great deal.

"This is disgusting," I announced to the Chief the following morning. "Obviously, this family doesn't appreciate anything I do."

With a determined stride, I headed for my Bible. Opening it right to Proverbs 31, I read about Her and the cushions and coverlets She made. I closed the book slowly and sat and thought. *Making cushions and coverlets will help me to control my anger. I've been angry twice now in a very short time.*

Fifty-one cushions, one crooked afghan, and three cranky children later, I realized I must have gone off the track somewhere.

No longer cruising along, I settled myself one morning for a good quiet time with the Lord. I reviewed the situation. First of all, John had removed the bumper stickers without a word. That hurt. And then, when I tried to tell him how to pray more effectively, he retreated behind his newspaper. Also, he had ignored the list of Bible verses I'd posted on the bathroom mirror so that he could memorize them while he was shaving.

The boys were unbelievably rowdy, and Specimen wasn't even glad to see me when she eventually returned home wearing a piece of somebody's garden fence.

I bowed my head in shame. "Obviously, Lord, I'm on the wrong track."

Sitting alone on the sofa, I opened my Bible again to Proverbs 31—and Her. Just after the part about cushions, I found that Her clothing was pure white. I recalled my white graduation dress and my pure white wedding dress seeded with tiny pearls. . . .

I must have dozed off because I heard shouts of, "Mom! Mom! Let us in! We're home from school!"

I carefully laid the Bible on the coffee table with the page marked for quick reference.

The rest of the day went more smoothly, but I didn't know why.

The next day, Saturday, John said he had business in town. I felt lonely, as though I'd drifted away from him. What had gone wrong, I realized while scrubbing the kitchen floor, was that *I* had created the distance between us by my critical spirit.

"Oh, God, I'm sorry—again," I whispered as my tears fell into the scrub water. I recalled with shame my childish behavior over the model railroad. "That's where it started," I said, rinsing the floor and putting away the cleaning supplies.

No sooner had I repented in my heart than my spirits began to lift. I thanked God for the tiny railroad which had brought so much happiness to John and the boys. I mused, *Even sincere Christians can jump the track now and then.*

Quick as a wink, I went straight to work. Gathering up the posters, the tracts, and the pillows, I stuffed them all into the hall closet with the rest of my skeletons of self-effort.

By the time John returned home, the kitchen was heavy with the scents of fresh apple pie and milk-fried chicken—his favorites.

"Something smells pretty good around here," commented my mate. He wrapped his arms around me and kissed me tenderly.

"Oh, John," I sobbed, "I'm truly sorry." No more words were necessary. He knew exactly what I meant.

"It's all right," he replied softly, smoothing my hair away from my face. "Come and see what I bought you today." He took me by the hand and led me to the kitchen table. A long, narrow box, wrapped in silver paper waited for me.

"Christmas is over," I said as I dried my eyes on my handkerchief. I opened it and discovered a white chiffon dress, delicately pleated, and trimmed with a suggestion of gold at the neck and waist. "It's beautiful!" I exclaimed as tears of happiness flooded my eyes.

"Open the card," he suggested, handing me a small, white envelope.

Fingers trembling, I ripped open the envelope and read the inscription which John had carefully written: "She has been permitted to dress in fine (radiant) linen—dazzling and white, for the fine linen is (signifies, represents) the righteousness—the upright, just and godly living [deeds, conduct] and right standing with God."[46]

Taking me into his arms, he whispered, "I found a verse of my own."

Te Deum—Thee, God, we praise.

MATT DRAKE

COMMENCEMENT

16 / Who?

"Charm can be deceptive and beauty doesn't last, but a woman who fears and reverences God shall be greatly praised."[47]

The cold, biting wind whipped through my coat as I stood staring in horror at the bridge washout which had claimed nine lives a week earlier. The winding mountain highway which led out of our town had done it again—snow melting high up in the peaks had created a great rock slide. It swept away houses, bridges and people into the murky depths of the ocean below.

Jean and I had been gone on a shopping trip in the big city. Although I'd seen pictures of the tragedy on television, I could hardly believe that such devastation had occurred close to home.

Standing there, actually viewing the gap gorged by the flash flood, I began to tremble. "Oh, Jean!" I pulled my coat around me and crossed my arms in front of me. "John will be traveling here next week. What if—?"

"Never mind the 'what if,' " replied Jean pulling me away and steering me back to our waiting automobile. "He's in God's care, remember?"

As I settled myself in the passenger side, Jean started the motor. Soon we were approaching the last long pull up and around the mountain before the road would dip and lead us into our valley. "Why don't we realize how brief life is?" Tears filled my eyes as I thought of those nine people.

"We don't like to think about our own mortality," Jean answered softly.

"I wonder how many of them were Christians?" It was a rhetorical question.

Jean stared at the road intently, concentrating on her driving. "Only God knows that," she responded in unison with my own thoughts.

Even after I'd arrived home, I couldn't shake the dread. Car after car sailing into nothingness, instead of crossing the bridge which was always there, was as graphic in my imagination as if it were happening again.

Terror for John's safety troubled me night and day. All too soon, he was ready to depart for his week of mayor meetings in several cities. John was eager for the trip. "It'll give me a break from teaching and some new ideas for our little city." He smiled, gave me a big hug and a kiss. Then he was gone.

The picture of the new temporary bridge flashed before me— heavy-duty equipment lifting gigantic boulders, and workmen in hardhats swarming like bees on a hive. I was glad the boys were in school as I turned slowly and trudged back into the house. Walking to the living room, I threw open the window and leaned out. The cold air felt clean against my cheeks.

The sky, a gray-blue, seemed lower than usual, and fog obscured my view of the Chief. A feeling of isolation enveloped me as I listened to the river that ran behind our house. I could hear the water slapping the rocks, dogs barking, a chain saw buzzing. But those normal sounds would never be heard again by those who had disappeared. They had been swept away into infinity.

We face the future, but we really don't, I thought, *and most of us fear the future.*

"Sometimes I fear it too, Lord," I prayed honestly. My whispered confession floated heavenward, and I closed the window and turned away from the view. I felt a chill in my bones.

A heaviness in my heart pressured me the rest of the day. I was thankful when the boys were finally settled in bed.

It had been months since a "dream attack" had sent its shivers through my system in the middle of the night, but I felt uneasy as I prepared to retire.

Ignoring the sensation, I climbed into bed. Sleep would not come. I realized I was in for a real battle. "Oh, no," I groaned, "a full attack is on the way." The signs marched over me with ferocity—vague discomfort in the vicinity of my brain, heart beating a little too fast now and then, sweaty palms. Soon the perspiration would form along my hairline, and then . . .

"And then *what?*" Sitting straight up in bed, and pulling covers up for warmth, I said, "I've never been awake during a full-blown attack. I don't know what comes next!

"I'm going to head right into this one," I promised myself. I hopped out of bed and grabbed a sweater from a hook in the closet. "First, I'll make myself comfortable. My feet are cold." Slipping my feet into fuzzy mules, I padded out to the kitchen, heated some water, filled a hot water bottle, and returned to bed.

I shoved the hot water bottle down to the end of the bed, and hauled the comforter up to my armpits. "There now," I announced to Her and to anyone else listening—nobody else was awake except Hampst, who loved to run at night—"I am ready for battle."

The clanging of the telephone on my night table bounced me off the mattress. "I knew it! Poor John!" I took a deep breath. "Hello?" I asked an unheard question. My voice shook.

"What's wrong with you?" Jean's familiar voice came through the receiver.

"I've been having strange attacks lately . . ." The words slipped out before I could stop them. I had never called them attacks out loud before.

"Attacks?" Jean's voice rose in alarm. "Are you all right? Shall I call a doctor?"

"Did I say *attacks?*" My tone mellowed out, "I must have been asleep when you called. You see, the phone is on the table right beside my bed and . . ." I trailed off hopefully.

"Oh," she sighed, "but don't scare me like that."

"Sorry," I replied honestly. "Why did you call?" I tried to sound happy and relaxed.

"I wanted to know what we're going to do in Bible study next week." From the sound of her voice, I was certain she had no idea of my real condition. I thought I heard crunching.

"Are you eating something?" I inquired while digging around on the night table for my Bible study notes.

"Uh, huh," she laughed, "popcorn."

I heard another mouthful join the other one. "I didn't know you liked popcorn," I commented. "It can be a dangerous habit."

"Oh," she giggled, "you mean I could get fat."

"That too," I replied sincerely. I wondered if she would ever have attacks about Her. *Does the popcorn come first, and then the assault on the senses, or does She drive women to popcorn?* I wondered.

"*Crunch, munch,*" she responded. "Guess I got it from you. It must be catching." Another chuckle.

I wanted to scream, "Don't eat it!" Instead I calmly reported my findings about next week's Bible study.

"It's all about God's deepening call to us. The example is Peter's faith when he learned to walk on the water to Jesus." I paused, "That is, until he stopped believing and started sinking." The words poured out of me like rice out of a full bag. I'd done my homework thoroughly and prayed for help besides.

"What I can't remember," said Jean as she chomped, "is how Peter finally got back into the boat."

"That's easy," I replied. "Jesus held out His hand and helped him, and—"

"Thanks, gotto go," she interrupted. "Bye." The click on the telephone reminded me that I was still alone for the battle with Her.

The thought of hot, buttery popcorn bombarded my brain as I tried to concentrate on Her. Try as I would, I couldn't seem to corral my mind to focus on the onslaught ahead of me.

"One tiny bowl never hurt anyone," I said, throwing back the comforter and scurrying to the kitchen.

Humming softly, I sniffed deeply as the yellow kernels began warming in the hot oil. Then the vigorous popping formed little steam clouds all around the lid. I delighted in the homey fragrance.

Plopping a blob of butter in the bottom of the pan, I watched with fascination as the chunk sputtered and melted into a yellow pool.

"Pure flavor," I said as I headed back to the bedroom with my snack.

"Mmmm, yum," I muttered as I munched contentedly.

The hot water bottle, the comforter, and the warm, buttery corn ganged up on me. I felt so sleepy . . .

. . . And then I was driving on the highway. The wind whipped the car from left to right, and I struggled to keep it on the road. Fog blurred my vision. Then it swirled around the headlights, forcing me to drive blindly. Mounting dread clutched me. Suddenly I felt the car leave the road—terror . . . blackness . . .

"Lord, save me!" I shouted as I found myself sinking in the sea.

Floundering to the surface, I gasped for air, and then a colossal wave swept me back down under the water. Panic mounted as I fought my way back to the surface. Breaking the water's hold, I forced my head above the spray.

"Come!"[48] the voice said.

I felt myself being lifted up and out of the water onto a soft surface.

". . . O you of little faith, why did you doubt?"[49]

Unable to see anything, I asked, "Are you Jesus?"

A voice said, "It is I; do not be afraid."[50]

I relaxed as a gentle peace washed over me and arrested my shivering terror. I tried to open my eyes, but I couldn't. *I must have been blinded in the fall,* I reasoned. Thankful that death had passed me by, I reached out my hand.

My fingers caressed something soft. Smiling in gratitude, I said, "Thank you, Lord Jesus. Why, this feels as soft as my comforter back home. I knew you would think of everything here!"

Suddenly my eyes flew open. "Home!" I exclaimed. Gradually I became alert. Rubbing my eyes, I looked around from a bed's-eye view.

"It was a dream," I told myself. *But not a dream attack,* my mind advised.

"That's right," I whispered into the empty room. "A dream *attack* always left me feeling lonely and low. I felt guilty when I compared myself to Her, a woman of strength and dignity. Not only that, She was pretty too," I recalled with chagrin.

But this time, my brain popped in, *Jesus was there.*

I remained awake until the wee hours sorting out what my dream had meant. I had obviously mixed up my Bible study lesson with my fears about John and the bridge washout. But this dream was different than any I had ever experienced. In the middle of my terror, in the midst of my struggle, Jesus was there with me.

"Wow!" I said to the half-empty popcorn bowl.

Ben, the guinea pig, heard my voice and began to whistle. He probably wanted a carrot.

Sitting in bed by myself, I prayed, "Oh, dear Lord, how wonderful it will be in heaven when I can hold your hand forever."

I closed my eyes in peace.

The next day I felt rested as I guided the children through their morning routine. I marveled at the calm which blessed my day. I wondered if I would ever have another dream attack. I longed to tell John about Her and me.

"No, I can't tell him—not now," I told myself. I did, however, vividly remember my meeting with the Lord Jesus Christ.

"When will Dad be back?" inquired George that night at bedtime.

"The day after tomorrow," I answered. I was as eager to see John as the boys were. I also looked forward to the Bible study the next morning about Peter walking on the water.

"You see," the pastor's face glowed with faith, "the call to Peter deepened until he was willing to give all he had—even his life—for his dear Lord."

"We have the same decision today, don't we?" I gazed intently into his eyes. If he said yes, then I had received my call!

"Yes." He looked at me strangely for a moment before he continued. "But Peter needed something more than commitment. He needed the power of the Holy Spirit. God sent that power to the believers on the Day of Pentecost."

I almost floated out of the room. I knew in my heart that

something important—even life-changing—had happened to me. But what?

When John arrived home the next day, I was thrilled to see him, but more quiet than usual. Later that evening, I explained my last dream to John. "I wonder what it means," I mused to him.

John held both my hands in his and listened intently. I was surprised that he gave me such rapt attention. Gently he responded, "Martha, I agree that a special moment has taken place in your Christian life. You should search your Bible for the true meaning of your experience. I will pray for you as you do."

"You're not laughing?" I questioned.

"Most certainly not." He responded with such sincerity that I was reminded of our wedding day.

Over the next few weeks She didn't bother me anymore at night, and I felt sure that She even was my friend during the day. I continued to search my Bible as John had suggested.

One morning, during my quiet time, the answer came.

All by myself in the house, I'd spent an unusually peaceful morning doing routine chores. And then Psalm 16:7 filtered into my thinking. Unable to recall it exactly, I looked it up in the Bible. "I will bless the Lord who has counseled me. Indeed, my mind instructs me in the night"(NASB).

Suddenly I knew the answer. During my dream, what I had heard in my Bible studies had come together in my subconscious. I recognized that only Jesus Christ could save me. Only Jesus could grant me freedom from all the snares of the Evil One.

I believed my dream was real because upon waking, the peace of Jesus Christ was still in my soul. I was experiencing the presence of the One who is the Beginning and the End, the Alpha and Omega.

Praise rose in my heart for Almighty God, and I prayed for a long time.

Over the following days, I hungered for the company of Jesus who would greet me one day in heaven. I wanted more than anything else to hear Him say, "Well done, thou good and faithful servant . . . enter thou into the joy of thy Lord."[51]

It seemed that in my dream Jesus Christ had asked me, as

He had asked Peter so long ago, "But who do *you* say that I am?"[52]

Even in my sleep, I knew the only answer possible for me. I responded, "Thou art the Christ, the Son of the living God."[53]

I could see the finish line ahead.

17 / Winning

"Her children stand and bless her; so does her husband. He praises her with these words: 'There are many fine women in the world, but you are the best of them all!' "[54]

"Just coffee this morning?" Puzzled, I turned off the stove, unplugged the toaster, and carried two cups of steaming black coffee to the kitchen table. "Do you feel all right, John?"

Ignoring my question, John hurriedly sipped the hot beverage as he skimmed through the paper. Then he shoved back his chair and left.

Happy birthday to me, I thought sadly.

"I will *not* give way to self-pity," I vowed. "He probably has a lot on his mind." I decided to make pancakes for the children. "They'll like that," I said hopefully.

While watching the boys inhale their breakfast, I inquired "Does anybody know why your father is walking to work in the rain?"

John Jr. glanced up only long enough to retort, "It's just misting."

George poured on another half cup of syrup, and Joe said, with a full mouth, "I want to get to school early."

"You want to go early—to *school*?" I couldn't believe my ears.

"Yeah. Want me to help you clear?" Joe offered.

"No. That's fine," I answered. Maybe at least Joe remembered my birthday, I noted mentally. "I'll get the car keys." All three piled into the car.

As I pulled up in front of the high school, John Jr. said his usual, "Bye, Mom. Thanks. Have a good day." He said it so fast—maybe that last phrase *was* "Happy birthday." No, I decided, he was too casual to have noticed the day.

"Bye, John," I responded, checking the rear-view mirror to be certain we wouldn't be wiped out by a speeding school bus.

"Bye, Mom," grunted Joe as he hauled himself out of the back and untangled his foot from the seat belt. No, he hadn't remembered.

"Bye, dear."

"Don't mash me!" screeched George from the passenger side of the front. When Joe pushed the seat forward, he'd folded George in—like a piece of baloney in a sandwich.

"Sorry," muttered Joe, shoving the seat back with a snap.

"Don't slam the door in my face!" shouted George as the heavy car door smashed shut.

"I hate sitting in the front," grumbled George, settling himself. I don't *think* he meant he hated sitting by me.

"Do you have the mail?" I asked

"What mail?" His blue eyes, framed by aviator glasses, squinted as he wrinkled his nose, giving an air of maturity to his otherwise blank expression.

"The stamped envelopes which I explained at the back door at home—bills that must be paid today. You said you would hold them until we arrived at the post office." I spoke slowly, trying to force down my feelings of irritation over his thoughtlessness. It was just one more snag in the morning's routine. Not only had everyone ignored my birthday, they all seemed even less friendly than usual.

"Oh," he replied, widening his baby blues, "*that* mail!" He twisted in his seat and began to scramble toward the back. "I must have left it somewhere."

"You must have left it at home," I countered, while looking for a place to turn the car around. "It's all right. It's still early. We'll get your boots too. It's starting to rain." I steered the automobile back home at a reasonable speed.

"It's just misting," argued my youngest darling.

"If it were 'just misting,' I wouldn't have to turn on the windshield wipers. As you can clearly see, I need them to see the road."

"Oh," he grumped.

Sensing that something was troubling him, I inquired, "What's the matter with getting your boots, George?"

"There's nothin' wrong with *getting* my boots," he fumed. "It's *wearing* 'em. I just love to wear gunboats so that people think my feet are bananas," he added sarcastically.

"Nobody wears overshoes this year?" I used a gentle tone. I realized that at his age, or any age, it hurts to be different. Pulling into our driveway, I could remember approximately ten pairs of clodhoppers I'd accidentally "lost" when I was his age. But then shoes didn't cost as much then as they do now.

"Do you feel that since nobody else protects his feet, you should be able to catch cold and ruin your sneakers?" I turned off the car motor, trying to keep a lid on my impatience.

"I didn't say that," he shot back. "I know you won't get me another pair for a whole year if I ruin these."

I am rather mean, I thought.

George stared miserably out of the car window.

"Tell you what," I offered, turning to face him. "Let us 'reason together,' as the Bible says. What would you suggest?"

"I will miss the puddles when I walk," he replied with his arms crossed and his eyebrows lowered.

"Can you do that?" I sincerely inquired.

"Sure!" he exclaimed eagerly. "And if I wreck my shoes, I can't get any for two years!"

"You're on," I answered. I'd learned a lesson from Her. Sometimes feelings of self-worth in the eyes of our peers are as important as saving shoes.

George ran in to get the mail. "Sorry I forgot," he said with real warmth when he returned to the car.

I didn't ask if he could also run between raindrops. I decided to leave the details to him.

After depositing him in front of the elementary school, I mailed the bills and returned home. I couldn't wait for my quiet time with God. I'd already received a few wounds today, and I knew that I wouldn't make it through the day the way She would unless I had some supernatural help.

I quickly cleaned up the kitchen, then sat down with my Bible and a little daily devotional book I'd been using.

"Brethren, I do not regard myself as having laid hold of it yet; but one thing I do: forgetting what lies behind and reaching forward to what lies ahead, I press on toward the goal for the prize of the upward call of God in Christ Jesus."[55] The verse for the day lifted me from my doldrums. Compared to the Apostle Paul, the forgetfulness of my family and George's ill temper were inconsequential.

I began quietly flipping at random through my Bible. Various slips of paper fell out. Carefully I unfolded little notes which I'd penned quickly and placed in my Bible for safekeeping.

"Pain will cause me to grow—like a caterpillar. The cocoon must cause depression and seem like an eternity. Therefore, I must learn to wait for God to change me so that I can be like Her." I'd written that nearly a year ago. I didn't see a difference in me, but I did notice a change in my surroundings. *I don't seem to hurt the same way*, I mused.

Before Her, I often felt bored, frustrated, and without purpose for no apparent reason. Now I realized that even discomfort has its purpose. "What's this?" I unfolded a piece of yellow tissue paper on which I had scribbled: "A husband is more than a paycheck, or a person to carry out the trash. I must learn to reverence my husband and honor him as my head—a little humiliation will lead me to humility." *I'm going to keep these notes for another year and see what's happening then*, I decided. I began to make a little pile of them.

On a facial tissue, I'd printed, "My children will do what I *do*, not what I say." I remember writing that when I thought I was suffering from mononucleosis. Tears of gratitude welled up in my eyes as I whispered, "Thank you, Lord, for bringing us through that time." The children had grown up a lot, not only in developing independence, but they had also learned the joy of serving another person.

Quickly I scanned the rest of the notations I'd made. Some

were carefully penned, others scribbled. All of them brought vivid memories of my struggle to be like Her.

"We become monsters when we mold ourselves. It's better to apply Rom. 12:2 to my life."

"The Bible is the best guidebook for raising children—Proverbs is especially good."

"She would never trust suntan lotion in the noonday sun, or the world for solace. She has more sense."

"If Her child brought a caterpillar into the house and placed it on Her houseplant, She would not yell."

"She would base her decisions on principle, not pressure."

"If Her son's sneakers had been stolen at school, She would pray for the thief and teach her child that prayer equalizes all situations by bringing in divine help."

"She probably spent the proper time in getting Her armor on (Eph. 6:11-17) *with prayer*." I recalled more than one time when I'd been *standing* on my shield of faith, unable to find my sword of the Spirit—the Word of God.

After reading each note, I gathered the pile and tucked it away in a sealed envelope. I marked the envelope "Private" and hid it in a secret place. "I'll read these again in a year," I promised myself. I knew I had just begun to scratch the surface in following Her example.

The time had come to complete my blouse. The decision calmed me. I was admitting the state of my soul, unfinished, and leaving the results to God.

As I rummaged around, gathering the blouse from the bottom of the hall closet, the sewing basket containing needles, pins, measuring tape, and other necessities, and setting up the machine, I recalled two verses from my Bible: (1) ". . . that out of his glorious, unlimited resources he will give you the mighty inner strengthening of his Holy Spirit."[56] (2) "But the fruit of the Spirit is love, joy, peace, patience, kindness, goodness, faithfulness, gentleness, self-control. . . ."[57]

"Well, Lord," I said as I faced the unfinished blouse, "it's just you and me . . ."

It might have seemed ridiculous to some, but I felt I needed someone to pray for me. I dialed Jean's number. She wouldn't make fun of me for asking her anything. She was my dearest friend, wasn't she? Certainly Jean would understand the seriousness of my request. I plunged right in as soon as she said hello. "Say, do you remember that blouse I was making?"

"Do I ever!" She laughed hysterically.

This wasn't going to be as easy as I thought. I waited for her to quiet down.

"Jean," I announced in a somber tone, "I can't face it."

"Why would you want to face it? As I recall, it had two sleeves, one crooked collar, and polka dots of oil." She muffled further snickers as she continued, "It doesn't need a facing!"

I waited for her to finish chuckling. "I am serious, Jean. I don't mean facing it, like putting in a lining. I mean approach the awful job of completing it. I know how ugly it looks. Will you pray for me?"

Suddenly serious, she replied. "Sure, I'll pray."

"Thank you," I responded and ended the conversation. I felt hurt.

"I really thought she would understand better," I said to myself as I sat down at the sewing machine. Why couldn't she have noticed how I was really feeling? I decided to let it pass.

Two hours later, after much effort and prayer, the blouse hung on a hanger in my closet. It wasn't perfection, but it was the best I could manage. I used snap fasteners instead of buttons, hemmed it on the machine with a zigzag stitch, scrubbed out the oil stains, and ironed it.

A basket of shirts waiting to be ironed reminded me that I had a lot of work to do before dinnertime. I hurried back to the sewing machine to clean up the mess. I realized I hadn't conversed with the Chief for a long time. I walked over and stood in front of the living room window. "What a lovely view. Thank you, God, for the majesty of your creation."

The Chief was really a gigantic cliff of granite rock consisting mainly of feldspar and quartz. Now he showed signs of spring. Pale green dotted the rock crevices. The sun sent rays of light streaming through the still-bare trees.

It was one of those special moments when the human mind almost, but never quite, comprehends the handiwork of Almighty God. Unknown to me, I had stopped talking to the mountain the day I'd realized that my real Chief, Jesus Christ, answered. Jesus was not a sleeping, silent mountain gazing into infinity—unseeing, unfeeling, and unaware. Jesus heard me, revealed himself to me through God's Word, and spoke to me through the Comforter He had sent, the Holy Spirit.

"Oh, God," I whispered, "despite all the unrest in the world, the confusion about what it means to be masculine or feminine, and the pollution of our world and our values, I know there is hope for anyone who will come to you."

The telephone rang.

"Martha," I heard Jean's familiar voice, "I'm sorry I laughed about your blouse. I did pray for you."

"Thanks," I responded warmly. "I somehow knew you would."

"What are you cooking for dinner tonight."

"Why?" I inquired.

"Last time you worked on your blouse, you forgot to cook dinner. I just thought I'd remind you."

"I probably would have forgotten today too. Thanks," I replied sincerely. It was her way of making amends.

"Where could I have put the roast for supper?" Stunned, I stood in front of the refrigerator staring at the empty second shelf. "Maybe I just *thought* I took it out of the deep freeze!" I ran down the stairs and opened the freezer lid.

"No roast?" I plowed through the bread, chicken, and various packages of fruits and vegetables. I searched frantically for the expensive piece of beef I'd planned for dinner.

I fought to remain calm as I climbed the stairs leading to the kitchen. A careful search through the entire refrigerator produced no beef roast. "I'll just have to fix pancakes and ask John if he knows about it, but what in the world would I have done with a whole beef roast?"

I walked into the living room. The rocking chair beckoned. I remembered all too well the time I used to spend there. "I need to iron," I said out loud. I'd read somewhere that one should pray for the person who wears the article of clothing being pressed. By late afternoon I had offered many prayers for John and John Jr., Joe, and George. I felt that heaven and their closets were richer for my labors.

"Hey, Mom! We're home!" Shouts from the back door informed me that three empty stomachs had arrived.

"What's for supper, Mom?" Joe's voice rose through the floor boards first.

I called them all together for a small meeting at the kitchen table. "Does anybody know anything about the beef roast for supper?"

Six blank eyes faced me.

"Well?" I carefully eyed each one. I really didn't think they would have taken it to school, but they might have loaned it to a friend or given one large dog a taste treat.

Six eyes looked down at the table.

"Humm," I said.

"May I do my homework now?" John Jr. inquired.

"What else can we have for supper?" asked George. I was certain he didn't have any information. All he wanted was food— the sweeter the better.

"Pancakes," I replied.

"Great!" he shouted. "Twice in one day! May we have tons of syrup?"

"Oh, all right," I answered. "Certainly you may go and do your homework."

The house seemed strangely silent. I had never seen the boys work so diligently on their lessons.

When John arrived home, I had the pancake batter prepared and the table ready for dinner.

"What's for dinner?" John inquired.

"Do you know anything about the roast?" I questioned.

"What's there to know?" he said as he headed for the living room.

"It's missing," I replied, following him.

"Oh," he replied in a monotone of disinterest. He grabbed the newspaper, sat on the sofa, and began to read.

Tears threatened to disclose the pain I felt, but I fought them. I was being treated worse than a hired maid. I wanted to shout, "It's my birthday! Doesn't anybody around here care?"

Instead I fled down the hall to our bedroom to pray. Softly closing the door behind me, I felt my eyes fill up and my vision blur. I tiptoed over beside the bed and knelt to talk to the only One who could help me.

"Oh, God," I began, lifting my eyes to the picture of Jesus which graced our wall, "I . . ."

"What's this?" My eyes widened in shock at the sight of my white chiffon dress, the one John had recently given me, laid out across the foot of the bed. In among the delicate pleats nestled a note, "Go to the living room."

I stood up, brushed away the telltale tears, smoothed my hair, straightened my skirt, and hurried out.

When I arrived in the living room, my three smiling sons held a sign in front of them which said:

This Certifies That
MOM
is
MOTHER
of the
CENTURY

John was grinning from ear to ear as he handed me a tiny white envelope. I hoped he wouldn't notice that I had been crying, but I saw the glimmer of pain in his deep blue eyes. He knew, and he was sorry.

"Happy birthday, Martha," John said softly, giving me a squeeze.

"Happy birthday, Mom!" shouted the boys.

"You didn't forget," I replied. Tears filled my eyes again and I could barely read John's careful script. "The roast is at the very bottom of the deep freeze. The boys are going to McDonalds. I'm taking you out to dinner. Please wear your white dress."

For once I was speechless. Like a schoolgirl, I raced back to our bedroom to change into the chiffon dress. I felt like an angel in a Christmas play as I donned the white frock trimmed in gold.

Just before I opened the door to join my husband, I knelt by the bed one more time. "Thank you, Lord," I whispered fervently, "for winning the war."

I wondered if She had ever been so happy.

18 / Finish!

"Praise her for the many fine things she does. These good deeds of hers shall bring her honor and recognition from even the leaders."[58]

"But *why* do I have to eat oatmeal?" George sat staring at his bowl as if he were wounded.

Yesterday's birthday celebration was over, and we were all back to normal.

"It's good for you," I replied firmly. "How about a few raisins on top?" I passed him the bowl filled with the sweet, dried grapes.

"They're ugly," he said, pursing his lips and propping his elbows on the table.

"I like it!" John Jr.'s enthusiasm raised Joe's eyebrows.

"Really?" My middle son shoved his full bowl smothered with raisins and sugar toward his older brother. "You can have mine!" He leaned over and patted John Jr's shoulder. "Maybe"— he turned charming brown eyes in my direction—"Mom will feel like whipping up a few eggs."

"Mom isn't so inclined," I responded, handing his bowl back to him. "Now get busy and eat while I read this Bible verse to you." Hearing no response, I suggested, "How about a few marshmallows on top?"

"Yeah!" they chorused.

I went to the kitchen cupboard, pulled out a bag of the white confections they would practically sell their bikes for, and returned to the table. "Okay," I announced. "Three each."

I settled myself to read while they struggled to swallow their cereal.

"Fix your thoughts on what is true and good and right. Think about things that are pure and lovely, and dwell on the fine, good things in others. Think about all you can praise God for and be glad about. Keep putting into practice all you learned from me and saw me doing, and the God of peace will be with you."[59]

I glanced around the table. John Jr.'s bowl was empty. Joe had nearly hit bottom, and George had waded through half of his.

"That's good enough," I said.

"Thanks, Mom!" exclaimed George as though he had been granted a stay of execution.

"Yeah," chimed in Joe.

"I heard that oatmeal sticks to your ribs," offered John Jr.

"How would you like a punch in yours?" Joe growled.

"All I said was that oatmeal is good for you." My oldest stuck out his chin defiantly.

"Can we stop this, please?" I rolled my eyes heavenward. "You won't even get to school at this rate, and I promised your father I'd get you there on time." I made eye contact with each one. "Can't you be thankful that it's Friday?" I took a deep breath and waited.

"Sorry," muttered Joe.

John Jr. busily checked his fingernails.

"John?" My tone informed him that I'd had enough.

"Sorry too," he mumbled.

"Good! We have that settled. Now I want your closest attention . . ." My smile faded. Joe had disappeared! I peered under the table and saw him perched in front of Hampst the Second's cage. "Joe, what are you doing?"

"Nuthin'," he replied in a muffled voice.

"Would you please return to the table and sit down? I am trying to conduct a small conference about this evening's activities."

"Oh, sure," he answered, his nose buried in his hamster's furry back. He climbed back into his chair, still holding Hampst.

"*Without* Hampst." I raised my eyebrows in warning and waited.

Joe spent what seemed like an eternity replacing Hampst in his cage, cooing and clucking to it all the while. "He knows his name now," he announced proudly as he resumed his position at the table.

Two down, I thought as I noticed the rapt attention of my eldest. George, however, had vanished.

"Where's George?" I asked in surprise.

Two blank faces tried to register a suitable emotion—like interest.

"George!" I shouted.

"What!" he yelled back from his room.

"What are you doing?" I increased my volume.

"I'm playing with Ben!"

I began to count to ten and pray at the same time. As soon as the thundercloud passed, I lilted musically, "George?"

"Coming!"

Returning, he challenged, "If Joe can play with Hampst, I can play with Ben."

I waited.

He sat down.

"Good," I said. "And now, about tonight . . ."

An hour later, after taxi duty to the schools, I stood elbow deep in dishwashing liquid, the one that "floated away everything"—except the oatmeal stuck on the bottom of an aluminum pot. "It doesn't budge it, let alone float it," I muttered, digging at the gummy mess with a pancake flipper. It bent. "I think I'll just let it soak for a while—like a couple of days," I joked. Noticing that the coffeepot was still half-full, I poured myself a cup.

"Break time," I announced to my crew of one. I carried my mug to the living room and flopped down on the sofa. The coffee was cold, but peace permeated my soul. I had been waiting for this moment of solitude.

Putting my feet up on the edge of the coffee table, I leaned my head back to remember the birthday dinner the previous evening.

I'd felt like an angel as John escorted me to a cozy restaurant where we had eaten by candlelight. It was one of those rare moments when we were transformed into sweethearts again. I thought he looked particularly handsome as he handled the waiter with self-assurance and ordered for both of us.

Between the main course and dessert, he presented me with a small box wrapped in silver paper. I tore off the wrap and peeked inside. I could hardly believe what I saw lying on soft velvet. "Oh, John!" I exclaimed in wonder.

"It's a little late, but it's your wedding present I couldn't afford." He beamed with manly pride.

Tenderly I fingered each pearl on the strand. My eyes misted as I opened his card and read, "There are many fine women in the world, but you are the best of them all!" (Prov. 31:29).

Tears leaped into my eyes, and I fought against the lump in my throat. The verse was about Her. My husband had honored me as Her husband had honored Her. I was speechless!

John reached across the table and took my hands in his. Searching my eyes for my feelings, he said quietly, "I have known for a long time . . ."

"About Her?" I couldn't believe it.

"About you," he corrected, "trying to be like the woman in Proverbs 31. It hasn't been too difficult to figure out." He smiled tenderly, his voice gentle.

"But how?" I felt a wave of relief flood over me at being discovered, but uncomfortable about being transparent. I wondered if the whole world knew about my struggles with Her.

"The butter stains in your Bible all over Proverbs 31, for one thing." He leaned back in his chair and grinned at his own sleuthing ability. "And then there were other signs I couldn't miss—like your sudden interest in sewing, gardening, making homemade jelly, and so forth. But one thing did puzzle me—"

"What?" I asked.

"What in the world were you doing with those red curtains?" His blue eyes twinkled with merriment.

"Oh, that!" I flushed with embarrassment. "That was so that my family would be be protected like Rahab's family was—you know, the scarlet cord out the window . . ." My voice trailed off.

"I like your theology, but the scarlet cord was a type of Christ's blood which protects us from eternal death. We don't need the type now when we have the real thing."

I flushed in discomfort. "I understand that now. Well, Skylab missed us anyway." I looked down at the string of pearls glimmering in the candlelight. "I didn't mean to keep it from you. About Her, I mean. I kept having an awful dream about being like Her. When I'd wake up, I'd feel guilty. I didn't want to bother you." Chagrin silenced me.

"Did you know that you talk in your sleep?" His mouth curved upward.

My eyes widened in horror. "You didn't listen!"

"No," he chuckled merrily. Leaning forward across the table, John whispered, "You are beautiful."

"Who, me?" My soft reply seemed to float from another galaxy.

I heard bells ringing from afar. I was Her . . .

Bells! The incessant jangling of the telephone snapped me out of my reverie. I hurried to answer it.

"What took you so long?" John's businesslike tone threw me for a moment.

"Oh, I was remembering a special dinner last night," I replied.

"Martha, I only have a couple of minutes before my next class."

"Oh," I answered good-naturedly.

"Is everything ready for tonight?"

"Yes, I spoke to the boys this morning. John Jr. will cook the pancakes for the three of them, and Joe—"

"That's good," John interrupted. "I don't want to be late. This get-together with the town council and their wives is important for the next election." He sneezed.

"Do you feel all right?" John never got the sniffles.

"I'm fine. See you then." And he hung up.

I spent the rest of the day preparing for the boys' supper at home, our dinner out, and my appearance. I spent a long time fixing my hair so that it softly framed my face. Then I manicured my nails and painted them an essence of pink.

"I think She would wear something simple, but tasteful," I

said as I rummaged around in my closet. It didn't take me long. I decided on my dark brown dress with a Peter Pan collar and matching pumps.

"Humm," I muttered, replacing the brown dress, "the pearls won't look nice with this. The neck is all wrong."

After yanking out all of my dresses and skirts, I finally decided the pearls would look best with black. "Basic black is always safe," I reasoned, carefully laying my one good black dress out.

By the time the boys arrived home from school, I was almost ready.

"Wow!" exclaimed John Jr. "You smell great!" He sniffed his way after me down the hallway until he hit the kitchen. He was pulled off my trail by the tantalizing odor of pancake batter and fresh maple syrup. "This smells even better," he grinned broadly as he stuck a finger in the batter.

"Leave it alone, Johnny. Now, are you *certain* you know how to handle this skillet? The thermostat can be tricky." I paused in uncertainty. I hated to leave the house and have the boys cooking without supervision.

"Stop worrying, Mom," John Jr. replied, patting me on the back. "We're going to be just fine!" He pushed me gently out of the kitchen. "Now you just go and finish getting ready. Dad hates to be late."

"I suppose you're right," I responded. "I can't baby you kids all your lives . . ."

By the time John arrived, I was ready and waiting.

"You look great," he said in between sneezes.

"You look sick," I replied.

I was concerned about the boys' safety and John's health, but we had to go. The party was to reward the town council for a year's hard labor and to create enthusiasm for continuing in work that often brought complaints from the public. The evening passed as well as could be expected, but John's face began to turn the color of wallpaper paste.

By the time we were driving home, I was positive he had the flu. It had been circuiting the schools in recent weeks. "John, as soon as we get into the house, please go to bed."

"I think I will," he agreed, rubbing his eyes. "I'm getting an awful headache."

"It's starting to rain," I commented as he turned on the windshield wipers.

"I know," he responded mechanically.

Swish, swash, sounded the rhythmic pattern of the blades going back and forth. *Swish, swash.*

Suddenly my eyes fixed straight ahead. I strained to see. "John! Look!" My hand clasped my mouth in terror.

"I see it," he replied, instantly alert.

Through the darkness I could see flashing red lights. "It looks as though . . ."

". . . it's in front of our house." My husband completed my sentence for me.

John pushed the accelerator almost to the floor, and in seconds we could see an ambulance, a fire truck, and a police car. I held my breath as my heart pounded out of control. John wheeled our car to the side of the road.

We leaped from either side of our automobile and ran toward the house, my feet getting soaked in the puddles. A rather large patrolman waved us back.

"We live here!" John shouted.

"Oh, excuse me," responded the embarrassed officer.

John ran ahead of me up the driveway and to the back door. Almost instantly he was knocked backwards into the carport. Specimen, her mouth full of pancakes, bolted for the backyard.

"John, are you all right?" I hobbled as fast as I could.

"Yeah," he replied, scrambling up and running into the house.

"Ma'am?" The husky voice of a burly fireman startled me from behind. I turned my ankle.

"Ow," I groaned. "What is it? Are the children all right? Was there—"

"Take it easy," he interrupted. "The fire is out. Your boys are all right, except for one who—"

My knees began to buckle. "Who what?" I squeaked.

"Who refuses to come into the house. He's still in the backyard with his hamster."

"Ohhh," I sagged against the wall. "I'll get him."

"Well," he looked around with practiced eye, "I guess we can leave now since you're home."

Knees quaking, stomach quivering, I limped out to the backyard. Way out, as far as he could get without landing in the river, sat a form which looked like a medium-sized boy. "Joe?" I called out.

"Mom!" he shouted excitedly. "Hampst could have been burned alive, but I saved him!" He ran as fast as he could toward me. He was soaking wet.

"Never mind," I answered in a thin voice. "Let's go into the house."

Pancake batter was everywhere! The wall with the outlet for the electric pancake skillet was charred from the fire. Maple syrup dripped from the table from where Specimen had obviously helped herself to pancakes.

John Jr. looked stricken, his face white from strain. George, however, beamed brightly. He was wearing his superhero cape.

It took the next hour to discover what had happened. By that time John was feeling so sick that I suggested he go to bed.

At 2:00 a.m., while I scrubbed the kitchen floor, I almost laughed.

I tried to imagine the whole scene in my mind. John Jr. had heated up the skillet. Then he had used about a cup of lard in order to "french fry" the pancakes—"a new taste treat."

When the grease caught fire, George had run to the telephone—unknown to John Jr.—and called the police (it was an emergency), the fire department (for obvious reasons), and an ambulance (just in case).

While John Jr. madly shook baking soda all over the kitchen to put out the blaze, George decided that all good dogs "save the day." So he called Specimen to the rescue.

Joe heard the fire engine siren and panicked. He grabbed his hamster and ran out of the house shouting, "I'm not losing another Hampst!"

During the scramble of firemen, policemen, and confused medics, the boys froze in terror at what John and I would think. And that, apparently, is when we arrived upon the scene.

By three o'clock in the morning, I had the kitchen in order

again. "I can wash the walls tomorrow," I said wearily to myself. I fell into bed, said a quick prayer of thanks, and was instantly asleep.

I awoke with a start. Glancing over at John, I saw that he was still slumbering soundly. I touched his forehead. It felt hot. Reaching for my robe, I wrapped it around me and tiptoed out of the room. Quietly I padded out to the living room in my mule slippers. Opening the drapes, I caught the first streaks of dawn's early light illuminating the Chief.

Since I no longer felt drowsy and the household was still in bed, I reached for my Bible. I sat down on the sofa and read, "I have strength for all things in Christ Who empowers me—I am ready for anything and equal to anything through Him Who infuses inner strength into me [that is, I am self-sufficient in Christ's sufficiency]."[60]

Joy welled up inside me. God had given me a verse to help me be like Her. Heaven-sent peace wrapped its gentle mantle around me. Finally I knew Her secret.

Notes

Awakening
  1. Proverbs 31:26, TLB
Nightmare
  2. Proverbs 31:16–18, TLB
Sewing
  3. Proverbs 31:19, AMP
Bible
  4. Proverbs 31:15, AMP
  5. Job 23:12, AMP
Lost
  6. Proverbs 31:10, AMP
  7. Ezekiel 34:16, NASB
  8. Luke 19:10, NASB
Beachhead
  9. Proverbs 31:20, NASB
  10. Jeremiah 1:18, 19, TLB
  11. Proverbs 31:27, NASB
Organization
  12. Proverbs 31:27, AMP
  13. Proverbs 31:17, NASB
  14. Romans 12:2, AMP
Skylab
  15. Proverbs 31:21, AMP

16. Joshua 2:18, AMP
17. Joshua 2:21, AMP
18. Hebrews 9:19–22, TLB

Plowing

19. Proverbs 31:16, AMP
20. Luke 9:62, NASB
21. Proverbs 31:16, AMP

Separation

22. Proverbs 31:12, AMP
23. Romans 7:24, NASB

Abide

24. Proverbs 31:13, 14, NASB
25. Proverbs 31:31, KJV
26. Psalm 91:1, NASB
27. Matthew 10:39, NASB
28. John 15:5, NASB
29. 1 John 2:6, NASB

Pruning

30. Proverbs 31:18, AMP
31. Job 1:21, NASB
32. Psalm 30:5, KJV
33. Job 23:10, NASB

Friendship

34. Proverbs 31:11, AMP
35. John 15:13, NASB
36. John 15:14, NASB
37. Proverbs 31:23, AMP
38. Proverbs 18:24, NASB
39. Proverbs 17:17, NASB
40. Proverbs 12:4, AMP
41. 1 Corinthians 11:7, AMP

Christmas

42. Proverbs 31:25, AMP
43. Titus 2:3–5, AMP
44. 1 Timothy 5:14, AMP

Thanks

45. Proverbs 31:22, AMP
46. Revelation 19:8, AMP

Who?
47. Proverbs 31:30, TLB
48. Matthew 14:29, NASB
49. Matthew, 14:31, NASB
50. John 6:20, NASB
51. Matthew 25:21, KJV
52. Matthew 16:15, NASB
53. Matthew 16:16, NASB

Winning
54. Proverbs 31:28, 29, TLB
55. Philippians 3:13, 14, NASB
56. Ephesians 3:16, TLB
57. Galatians 5:22, 23, NASB

Finish!
58. Proverbs 31:31, TLB
59. Philippians 4:8, 9, TLB
60. Philippians 4:13, AMP